AN INTRODUCTION TO
HOMER

D0361118

AN INTRODUCTION TO

HOMER

W. A. CAMPS

CLARENDON PRESS · OXFORD
1980

Oxford University Press, Walton Street, Oxford OX2 6DP

OXFORD LONDON GLASGOW
NEW YORK TORONTO MELBOURNE WELLINGTON
KUALA LUMPUR SINGAPORE JAKARTA HONG KONG TOKYO
DELHI BOMBAY CALCUTTA MADRAS KARACHI
NAIROBI DAR ES SALAAM CAPE TOWN

Published in the United States by
Oxford University Press, New York

British Library Cataloguing in Publication Data

Camps, William Anthony
    An introduction to Homer.
    1. Homer – Criticism and interpretation
    I. Title
    883'.01   PA4037   79–42912
    ISBN 0–19–872099–8
    ISBN 0–19–872101–3 Pbk

Printed and bound in Great Britain by
Morrison & Gibb Ltd, London and Edinburgh

PREFACE

This book is in two parts. The first is an essay on the character of Homeric poetry and the ingredients of its effectiveness. The second is an assembly of notes and supplementary matter, arising from what is said in the essay and intended to explain, illustrate, or elaborate particular points. The principal purpose of the book is in the first part, and will not be frustrated if the contents of the second are read selectively, or neglected altogether.

The *Iliad* and the *Odyssey* are widely read in translation, far more widely indeed nowadays than they are in Greek. They can be thoroughly enjoyed in translation; and the essay which follows will try to suggest some reasons why this is so. Nevertheless, an important component of their excellence is necessarily lost in translation, being a product of certain properties of the Greek language, and of the Homeric metre, which English is not able to share. To give the Greekless reader some idea of this, Greek words will be quoted here and there in English spelling. Anyone who finds the result distasteful, or unhelpful, or both, can safely skip the passages in question. The book is addressed primarily to others than classical scholars or professional students of Homer. If nevertheless some of these latter find parts of it worth their attention, the author will be pleased beyond his expectations.

Very many books about Homer exist already, and the only justification for this one is that its approach to the subject is different from, and simpler than, that of most others. A useful and informative bibliography has been provided by J. B. Hainsworth in the series called *New Surveys in the Classics* (No. 3, *Homer*, 1969). Answers to most questions will be found in the *Companion to Homer*, edited by A. J. B. Wace and F. H. Stubbings (1962), and in G. S. Kirk's notable book *The Songs of Homer* (1962). The excellent *Introduction à l'Iliade* in the Budé Library, edited by Paul Mazon (1942) is primarily of technical interest: but Mazon's own concluding words on pp. 299-9 have a universal appeal. Anybody who has not read Matthew Arnold's two essays *On Translating Homer* will surely not regret now doing so.

Most generous help has been given by Mrs A. M. Morgan, Messrs

C. G. and N. Wilcockson, Professor M. M. Willcock, Mr L. P. Wilkinson, and a critic who remains anonymous. It is a pleasure as well as an obligation to render thanks to all of these.

W. A. C.

Cambridge
June 1979

CONTENTS

PRELIMINARY

Nobody knows who Homer was, or where or precisely when the *Iliad* and the *Odyssey* were made. That they were made after the beginning of the iron age is clear from fairly frequent references to the use of iron that occur in them. It is clear also that they preserve impressive memories of an earlier age, when weapons were of bronze and places later insignificant, such as Mycenae and Pylos, were centres still of wealth and power. The tale of Troy is told in the *Iliad* as one of great events long past and of men far greater than those the poet and his hearers knew.[1]

There is good reason to believe that the *Iliad* and the *Odyssey* were known—indeed, were publicly recited—at Athens in the second half of the sixth century BC.[2] That was fifty years, perhaps, before the first plays of Aeschylus were exhibited, some 500 years after the beginning of the iron age. The quality and character of the poems suggests that they were created late rather than early in the span of those 500 years; but this is no very firm foundation for conjecture.[3]

The poems purport to tell of events that attended or followed on a great war fought by bronze-armed men from all over Greece, led by the king of Mycenae, against a strong town called Troy, near the south shore of the Hellespont at its western entrance. Was there really such a war? Here three things only need be said. First, it is prima facie unlikely that a story so circumstantial as the Homeric tale of Troy should have had no origin in fact at all. Second, the history of the heroic poems of peoples other than the Greeks shows that the memory of real events is apt to be magnified and transformed almost beyond recognition in the telling and retelling of them over a span of several generations.[4] Third, excavation has shown that in the bronze age there stood indeed where Homer says Troy stood (and the town called Ilium stood in Roman times) a strong-walled city which was utterly destroyed by fire in the latter part of the thirteenth century BC.[5] It is a fair conjecture that there was a 'Trojan War', but that it was very different from the account that we have in the *Iliad*, in which memories of more than one period of time, and perhaps of more than one adventure, have become amalgamated as the story was told and told again.

It must have been by word of mouth that the blurred but persistent memory of that war, and of the bronze-age world in which it took place, was handed down to the generation in which the *Iliad* and *Odyssey* was made; since for much if not all of the intervening period the art of writing did not exist in Greece. What did exist was a class of professional story-telling poets, representatives of which appear as characters in the *Odyssey* itself. The repertories of these story-tellers must normally have consisted of pieces of relatively brief duration, adapted in length to the requirements of an evening's entertainment or the like. Such pieces could of course be strung together readily enough to form chains of successive episodes, as long perhaps or longer than our *Iliad* or *Odyssey*. What distinguishes the *Iliad* and the *Odyssey* is the combination in each of extensive scale with compact and organized and aesthetically satisfying overall design.

SIMILARITIES AND DIFFERENCES BETWEEN *ILIAD* AND *ODYSSEY*

The two poems exhibit evident similarities in their language and style, in the manner in which their incidents are presented, and in the combination of unity with magnitude which distinguishes their construction. They exhibit differences also. The *Iliad* is simpler in design, less diversified in its subject matter, and more intense. The *Odyssey* is more ingeniously organized, more widely ranging, and on a lower emotional level. Some scholars think that one man made both poems; and others think that this cannot be so. The matter is one of personal opinion: no proof is possible, either way.

The *Iliad* sets out its story in a simple chronological sequence; and while this sequence is for the most part logical as well as chronological—its incidents arising from one another and not merely succeeding one another—there are traces still of a presumably primitive concern for symmetry in the repetition of certain motifs, accompanied sometimes by unconcern about the logical requirements of their context.[6] The *Odyssey* on the other hand is put together somewhat in the manner of a periodically constructed complex sentence: the

principal strand of the narrative interrupts itself to admit a long retrospective parenthesis, and has prefixed to its beginning the beginning
of a subordinate strand which will later be brought into combination
with it.

The physical setting of the human action of the *Iliad* is limited
to camp, plain, and beleaguered town; and its cast of human characters
consists (with few though important exceptions) of fighting chieftains
and their fighting men. In the *Odyssey* the characters are very widely
diverse in their conditions and relationships—princes and beggars, fond
parents and cherished offspring, giant, witch, and fairy, nurse and
foster-children, mistress and maids, brutal villain and sly villain, faithful retainers, temperamental or eccentric old gentlemen, and so on.
And this diversity of persons is matched by the diversity of places
which the story visits: lordly mansion, idyllic grotto, enchanted palace,
giant's cave, witch's house in the woods, swineherd's hut, and Odysseus'
own house with its several apartments, and the island of Ithaca with
its several distinctive landmarks.

The *Iliad*, though it sees its heroes as far surpassing in their capacities 'men such as men now are',[7] derives its story from events which
in kind are all too plainly recognizable as coming within the range of
real human experience—a fatal quarrel between two great men and a
series of battles between two warring armies. It depicts reality magnified and intensified. The *Odyssey* on the other hand derives its story
from motifs of fable—the return of the husband unrecognizable or
disguised, the 108 importunate suitors, the wife's subterfuge of the
weaving that is daily done and nightly undone—and develops the story
thus derived in terms of real human experience. It dresses fable in
reality. This illusion of reality is not disturbed by a retrospect of
earlier very manifestly fabulous adventures of the hero, which are
ingeniously introduced in a parenthesis.

The *Odyssey* looks back with grief and regret to the war at Troy,
notwithstanding the victorious outcome of that war, to which the
Iliad looks forward. And this sentiment is not confined to the members
of Odysseus' household and the Ithacan fathers who have lost their
sons. The surviving victors Nestor and Menelaus are thinking always
of their fallen friends; and when Odysseus hears the Phaeacian bard
sing of the taking of Troy, he, the victor, is moved to tears, and our
poet likens his tears to those of a woman in a taken town who clings
to her dead husband's body while her captors prod her with their spear
butts and drag her away to be a slave. But even in the *Iliad*, though
there is joy of battle as well as agony, and admiration of warlike skill

and courage, there is no glorification of war as such. The war is seen by men on both sides as a calamity visited on them by fate or gods;[8] and the victories of Hector over Patroclus and of Achilles over Hector are told as hollow triumphs for the victors.

THE WORLD OF THE POEMS

The stories told in the *Iliad* and *Odyssey* are based on stories handed down over several generations, for they preserve (as we have seen) memories of an already quite far distant past. It is thus not possible to assume that the conditions of life which they depict correspond exactly to those of any single period: their world is the world of an accumulative tradition, familiar to the poet and his audiences partly from old tales, and not required by them to correspond in all respects to their own contemporary experience. What follows needs to be read with this reservation in mind.

The 'people', free but unprivileged members of the community, will have comprised of course the majority of men; but we do not hear much about them. Most of them, when not at war, will have been engaged principally as small-holders in tilling the soil and keeping a few beasts. Some landless men we find working as labourers for a wage. Others, more fortunate, are attached as retainers in various capacities, and in various ranks of dignity, to men of substance. These men of substance form a kind of aristocracy. They have more land and cattle and bondservants and other possessions, acquired partly by inheritance and partly as booty from war and forays as well as by other means. Above them in each community is one who is their head, perhaps as a firmly established overlord, perhaps as inheritor by custom of a primacy which may be either readily or precariously acknowledged. There exists also a small category of craftsmen and professionals: metal-worker, wood-worker, physician, bard, seer. Sometimes one can see how a physical disability encourages the development of a skill: a lame man can be efficient as a blacksmith, a blind man as a bard. Finally there are bondmen and bondwomen, the latter more numerous than the former because when taken as spoils of war they are preserved for their general usefulness, while men, being more dangerous, are apt to be preserved only if a good ransom is in prospect. The men in bondage of whom we hear are farm-hands or herdsmen; and some of the latter in remote pastures have much independence and responsibility.

Power in the community rests eventually with the few, the men of substance, unless one among them has acquired an overwhelming preponderance; where this is not so they may nevertheless be amenable to the prudent and tactful leadership of a 'king' whose position is hereditary but whose power is less than absolute. The 'people' are summoned from time to time to an assembly, as soldiers on a campaign or as citizens in peace-time. They possess no initiative, but their col-lective sentiment when thus assembled is something of which their superiors have to take account. In assembly all are free to speak their minds, but anyone who does so without power behind him may find himself bullied or chastised.

Marriage between the unfree is arranged by their masters. Between free citizens, at least in the higher strata of society, the custom is for the suitor to make gifts to the family of the woman whose hand he seeks. He does not expect her to bring a dowry with her; though it appears that sometimes gifts do pass from her family to him.

The simplest form of dwelling consists of a hut, to which may be annexed some kind of roofed shelter set against its outer perimeter, or a fenced yard, or both. A great man's house is an elaboration of this. The hut is magnified into a great hall, approached through a fenced or walled courtyard, with a portico on one or more sides. It has an-nexed to it several private chambers, and a separate apartment for the women, possibly upon an upper storey. We hear also of a store-room, and of a bathroom with several bath-tubs built into it. The large houses are impressionistically described, so that it is not possible to construct a clear and consistent picture of any of them in detail: they may indeed combine features inherited from more than one earlier version of the tales in which they occur.

Life in these houses centres on the great hall, in which the masters and their retainers take their meals, and drink and talk at leisure, and are entertained by bards who tell their stories in song to the ac-companiment of the lyre. A fire burns on a principal hearth, pro-ductive doubtless of a great deal of smoke. Supplementary illumination at night is provided by pinewood brands, set in or fed from some sort of braziers. Food at table consists mainly, if not wholly, of roasted meat with wheaten or barley meal in one form or another as adjunct. Carving and serving of food and wine at meals in the hall is done typically by male retainers; but senior women servants are the ones regularly called on to offer the first refreshments to guests of distinction. The women of the household, including the mistress, spin and weave; and this work is incessant, for the production of cloth from raw wool by hand is an immensely slow and laborious business. Skill in the making of finely textured or patterned material is highly prized. The serving women also sweep and clean and—another very laborious task—fetch water from sometimes quite distant sources for all the needs of the household. Nursing the mistress's children, dispensing the stores, and supervising the work of their juniors are other duties of the more responsible among them.

The daughters of the family take a part in some of the domestic work, notably the laundering of clothes, which is done outside the house in troughs located near a spring or stream. In old-fashioned families the daughters may also assist a distinguished visitor when he takes a bath. The men too of such families may take a hand in outdoor work, ploughing and reaping and herding beasts: they may also excel in some of the skills proper to artisans such as carpentry, and a nobleman as well as a bard may play the lyre and sing heroic stories to it.

Feasting, hunting, and athletic sports are favourite pastimes of the well-to-do. Young men and women of all conditions are practised in the art of dance.

All are well acquainted with the sea, which is a principal means of traffic between communities. Islanders move their cattle by ship from one pasture-ground to another. Some men sail the sea for trade; though the merchants most often mentioned are Phoenicians rather than Greeks. Some sail the sea as pirates and marauders.

For the world of the *Odyssey* as well as that of the *Iliad* is a world that is rough and unruly. Towards those outside a man's community few obligations are recognized. Armed aggression for some is a way of life, necessary to them for their own survival. Piracy and kidnapping and cattle-lifting are not disreputable occupations. The vanquished, if not ransomed, must expect to be killed or enslaved. Passions are violent. Yet pity for the helpless and respect for the fallen are sentiments after all held in honour, as also are courtesy, generosity, and hospitality.

Within the community there are rights of property and person that are clearly established by custom. But unless there is present an authority that happens to be both just and powerful, the maintenance of a man's rights depends on his own ability to defend them: law and public opinion will do no more than authorize action that he takes on his own behalf by way of self-defence or in reprisal. In the *Odyssey* the absence of the hero has left the Ithacans without a presiding authority. His son appeals to his fellow-citizens at a town-meeting to check the licentious proceedings of the uninvited guests who are consuming his substance. But those who speak up for him are put down by the other party and the meeting breaks up without result.

Homicide within the community, voluntary or involuntary, is left to the family of the slain men to avenge. This they do by killing the killer, unless he escapes them by becoming an exile, or they agree to accept, as sometimes happens, a price in compensation.

For the poor man—and shipwreck or other accident may reduce anyone to this condition at any time—the importunate demands of the belly are an all-absorbing preoccupation, as the hero of the *Odyssey* has learned by experience, and more than once remarks.[9] For the more fortunate the ruling preoccupation is with 'honour',[10] of which wealth and position are conditions, but of which they are by no means the sole constituents. Wealth stands in a peculiar relation to honour, in that gifts are symbols of respect, and that compensation for insult may be exacted or accepted in terms of material payment: for this reason a concern for honour may sometimes be difficult to distinguish from an appetite for gain. Honour is of supreme importance because a man's sense of his own worth is affected naturally by his awareness of the judgement passed on it by others; and the confidence of a man's own worth is what, for a hero, gives his life itself its value. Honour is diminished by any infringement of a person's rights or denial of his legitimate expectations (e.g. of the recognition of a past service rendered, or the granting of a justified request). Honour is enhanced by the possession and exercise of personal qualities that are exceptionally esteemed for their usefulness to their possessor and to the community: chief of these are courage and strength and military and athletic skills, also resourcefulness and persuasive speech, and, to a lesser extent, physical beauty. These gifts will be anyway admired, but the admiration will be lessened if they are not allowed to benefit a man's people and his friends: the selfish use of high capacities is a matter for reproach. And admiration will be lessened further if a man is felt to be lacking in respect for the opinions and feelings and interests—in fact for the 'honour'—of other men.[11] Achilles in the *Iliad* fails gravely twice in this respect. But we have the word of the king of the gods himself that the failure is a temporary aberration.

THE SUPERNATURAL

Supernatural powers are at work everywhere and always in the Homeric poems, causing things to happen which modern man would suppose to be due to known material causes, or human character, or simple chance. This view of things continued indeed to prevail in the pagan world of much later times. If an arrow luckily strikes the best protected part of a fighter's body, a friendly god may have guided it. If a man's bowstring breaks at a critical moment, or the fastenings of his armour come away, an unfriendly god may have been at work. A stroke or a heart attack, an epidemic, a storm at sea, an invasion by marauders—these are all the doing of a god or gods. A sudden access of confidence or energy or impressiveness (or, conversely, of fear), a momentary paralysis, an attack of overmastering desire or anger, an unaccountable error of judgement, an apparently unmotivated impulse—all these too may be thought of as due to some supernatural compulsion. Not all such things are attributed at all times to supernatural influence, but this is commonly the case if the occurrences are impressive in themselves or have important consequences. An incidental result of this way of seeing and explaining things is that the difference between the probable and the improbable is less strongly felt than it is in a world in which human or material causes are assumed to be responsible for most events and luck responsible for the rest. Gods can work miracles, great ones as well as small. Less wonder then that a man can pass unseen past sentries and through barred doors, if a god is there to manage the proceeding.

For the people for whom the *Iliad* and *Odyssey* were made these active and ubiquitous powers must have been invisible and as a rule unidentifiable. And this as a rule is true of the people in the stories also. A man whose bowstring snaps at a critical moment, or who is dismayed by the unexpected reappearance of someone thought long lost, will declare that this must be the doing of 'a god' without professing to know what god it is. Sometimes indeed the gods to achieve their ends disguise themselves as mortals known to people in the story. Only conjecture then or a special gift of perception will let their true identity be known, unless, as sometimes happens, they reveal it of their own accord. But they appear also in the stories in quite another way. Long before the *Iliad* and the *Odyssey* came to be made the imagination of poets had begun to endow the gods in their own identities with human forms and personalities and attributes, and to depict them thus conceived not only in their interventions in human affairs—sometimes visible only to the poet and his audience, sometimes to the human participants in his story too—but also in their life among themselves in their own abode, their domestic relations and discussions and disputes.[12]

From this conception of the gods as human in form and mentality (though superhuman in power and exempt from the human destiny of death) there results a perspective which sets the quality of the human agents in relief. Because of their nearness to and converse with the gods the heroes are seen—as 'men such as now men are' cannot be—as peers of the gods themselves in strength and splendour. Because of their mortal condition they acquire—as carefree and immortal gods cannot—the moral dignity of effort and endurance. This sense of the kinship and contrast between men and gods illuminates the poet's picture of his heroic world. More will be said later also of particular effects of variety and intensity which his gods contribute to his stories.

But it is time now to outline the content of these stories, telling them, as they can be told, essentially in human terms.

THE STORY OF THE *ILIAD* IN OUTLINE

A confederacy of Greek peoples is besieging the town of Troy. The siege is in its tenth year. A quarrel breaks out between Agamemnon, overlord of the confederacy, and Achilles, its most effective fighter in the field. Agamemnon takes from Achilles a prize of honour earlier awarded to him, and by this Achilles' honour is gravely affronted. He responds by withdrawing his services—he is a volunteer—and he prays that defeat in the field may humiliate Agamemnon and enhance his own value (honour) as his prowess comes to be appreciated as indispensable.

His prayer is granted. Battle begins. The first day's fighting (rich in episodes which have little coherence but considerable introductory value in relation to what follows) is inconclusive. But when after a day's interval the fighting is resumed the Trojans led by Hector (son of their king, Priam) get the upper hand. At nightfall they decide to bivouac on the battlefield, with high hopes of a decisive victory next day.

Agamemnon is now thoroughly alarmed, and admits his error. At the suggestion of Nestor, his senior adviser and a person of great age and experience, he sends honourable envoys, some of Achilles' closest friends, to appeal to him to come to the rescue, and to offer him restitution of the prize taken from him and abundant gifts in compensation for the insult done him. But Achilles, obsessed with his grievance, is obstinate. He rejects Agamemnon's amends and his friends' appeal.

The battle is resumed. The Trojans' victorious progress continues. One after another most of the principal champions of the Greeks are wounded and disabled. The Trojans storm the wall of the Greek camp, and carry the fighting into the camp itself. The Greeks make a brief recovery and drive them out; but soon the tide turns again and the Trojans fight their way into the camp for the second time and press forward to destroy the invaders' ships. Meanwhile Achilles' squire and friend Patroclus has been urged by Nestor to try himself to persuade Achilles to relent. Reproaching Achilles for his inhumanity he pleads urgently with him. Achilles is prisoner of his own earlier refusal, but he allows Patroclus to borrow his armour and lead their men out to save the ships, warning him to turn back once this has been accomplished. Patroclus saves the ships and routs the Trojans. But he forgets the instruction given him. He pursues his success too far and is killed by Hector beneath the wall of Troy. After a fierce struggle his friends bear his body back to the Greek camp.

When Achilles hears of Patroclus' death he is plunged into a frenzy of grief, remorse and rage. His anger against Agamemnon is suddenly and completely forgotten, replaced now by a far fiercer anger against the man who has killed his friend. Reconciled with Agamemnon and armed in new and splendid armour (gift of a god) to replace that lost with Patroclus he rides out in fury to find Hector and kill him. He and we know that by this he will hasten his own death too, for it is fated that his own death shall follow soon on Hector's.

Meanwhile Hector, made over-confident by his late success and unwilling to relinquish the hope of final victory that has come so very near to fulfilment, has brusquely rejected the advice of a friend that the Trojans should retire into their city and not attempt to offer battle in the new situation created by Achilles' return to the field. In consequence his people are routed by Achilles with fearful slaughter. The survivors escape into the city. Hector, remorseful and ashamed, stands alone outside the wall to face Achilles, watched from above by his father and mother and fellow-citizens with agonized apprehension. They fight and Hector falls. Achilles drags his body behind his chariot round the walls of Troy and back to the Greek camp.

Achilles gives Patroclus a splendid funeral. But his hatred and anger against Hector remain unappeased. He lets his body lie unburied and subjects it to persistent insults. Even the gods are indignant and disgusted.

But Priam, Hector's father, is inspired to go alone into Achilles' presence and beg to be allowed to ransom his son's body. He puts Achilles in mind of his own father, Peleus, an old man like himself, comfortless far away. Achilles' anger melts suddenly, turned to sympathy. He accepts the ransom and gives Priam what he asks, treating him with kindness and courtesy. Priam takes the body of Hector back to Troy, where his people honour his memory and give him a funeral worthy of his merits.

THE STORY OF THE *ODYSSEY* IN OUTLINE

Long years have passed since Troy was taken and the victors of the siege set out for home. But Odysseus, ship-wrecked after many adventures on his homeward way, has remained ever since marooned on a distant island, cherished prisoner of the sea-nymph Calypso. She loves him dearly and has offered him the gift of immortality. But he longs to return to his wife and his home.

At *Odysseus'* home in Ithaca meanwhile most people have given him up for lost. In consequence rival suitors are pestering his wife to remarry, partly because of her own attractions and partly with an eye to advancing a claim to Odysseus' royal prerogatives. Abusing the customary entitlement of visitors to hospitality they are making themselves free of Odysseus' house and eating and drinking daily at his expense. Odysseus' son Telemachus, a boy till now, has been powerless to prevent them. When the story of the *Odyssey* begins he is just emerging into manhood. His mother Penelope, as we presently learn, longs and still hopes for Odysseus' return, and the thought of marriage to any other man is repulsive to her; but her hope is fading, the pressure on her is increasing and her resources for resisting it are nearing exhaustion.

Two developments now take place, roughly simultaneously with one another. Telemachus suddenly decides to assert himself as a man and head of the household. And Calypso consents at last to let Odysseus go.

Telemachus warns the suitors (of course without effect) to leave the house, making them responsible for the consequences if they do not. Then he sets out by ship for the mainland in quest of some definite news of his father, alive or dead. From Nestor at Pylos and Menelaus at Sparta he hears the stories of what befell the other Greek chieftains after the fall of Troy, and a report that his father is alive but captive on an island far away. The suitors in Telemachus' absence plan to ambush and kill him on his way back to Ithaca.

Meanwhile on Calypso's island far away the nymph has at last been persuaded to let Odysseus go. With her help he makes a raft, and sets out in it across the sea. After some days of uneventful sailing a violent storm arises. The raft is wrecked, and Odysseus escapes with difficulty by swimming, to come ashore at last in the land of the Phaeacians, where King Alcinoüs receives him kindly and promises to have him carried safely home to Ithaca. In Alcinoüs' palace he tells his hosts (at length) the story of all his past adventures since leaving Troy (the encounters with giants and witches and sundry marvels that make up the best known part of the whole poem).[13] That done, the Phaeacians with magical speed convey him, sleeping, home to Ithaca and land him in a remote part of the island.

Disguised and accoutred as a tattered castaway, Odysseus now finds shelter (unrecognized) in the hut of his own head swineherd, from whom he learns how things stand with his family and in his home. Presently Telemachus, returned from his travels after escaping the suitors' ambush, comes to visit the swineherd. While the swineherd is temporarily absent Odysseus sheds his disguise and reveals himself to his son. Together they plan their next move. Odysseus resumes his disguise.

Next morning he proceeds to his own house in the Ithacan town, and enters it in the character of a beggar seeking alms. He observes, and himself suffers from, the arrogant and brutal behaviour of the suitors. He waits for his chance. He dare not yet reveal himself even to his wife, with whom as mistress of the house he is invited to a private conversation. More than once he is in danger of premature recognition. The tension rises.

Penelope, not recognizing her husband in the tattered stranger, and seeing that her son is now grown up and able to take his place as his father's heir, decides (or appears to decide) that she must at last surrender to the suitors' importunity.[14] She proposes a test to settle who shall have her hand and take her to his home. The test is, to string Odysseus' bow and perform with it a certain feat of archery. The bow is brought. The suitors try in turn to string it, without success. Penelope leaves the hall. The bow comes presently, despite protests from the suitors, into the hands of Odysseus himself.

The dénouement follows swiftly. The suitors, taken unawares, are killed to a man by Odysseus, helped by his son and two loyal servants to whom after cautious sounding he has already revealed himself. He sheds his disguise and resumes his natural appearance. Penelope, afraid at first to believe that her wish has at last come true, now sees him as she remembers him, and the recollection of a shared secret seals their reunion. They tell one another, as they lie in bed together, what has happened to each during their long separation; and Odysseus tells Penelope of further trials prophesied for him, though with final homecoming and a quiet end at the last: the poet's tact thus tempers his happy ending with a touch of bitter in the sweet. On the next day peace is made between Odysseus and the families of the men on whom he took his vengeance.[15, 16]

OMISSIONS FROM THE OUTLINES

These summaries have concentrated on the central themes of the two poems. They would be misleading without some indication of what they omit. First, they give, naturally, no idea of the diversity and interest of the episodes that arise in and from the development of the central themes themselves. Secondly, they give no idea of the large *proportion* of the whole extent of each poem which is given to matter incidental to these central themes, though relevant and sometimes necessary to them: more than half of the *Iliad* is occupied by the long battle scenes from which the hero on account of his withdrawal is wholly absent, and nearly a fifth of the *Odyssey* is occupied by the tales told in retrospect, by Nestor and Menelaus and Odysseus himself, of events and adventures long since past at the time of telling. Thirdly, they omit all reference to the considerable part played in the stories by the Homeric gods, whose directing purposes—of Zeus in the *Iliad* and Athena in the *Odyssey*—emphasize the organic character of the wholes, and whose supernatural powers make possible developments which could not with plausibility be presented otherwise, such as the entry of Priam unobserved into the Greek camp and Achilles' quarters at the end of the *Iliad*, or the changes that make Odysseus in the *Odyssey* alternately unrecognizable or recognizable as the story requires. As commenting spectators or as active participants the gods also at some moments enhance the pathos of the human story. They also, in the *Iliad* especially, relieve its tension occasionally by appearing as dramatis personae in scenes of homely or even farcical comedy.[17]

UNITY OF DESIGN

The outlines of the stories have, perhaps, been made clearer by these omissions. But they have not been falsified; and the fact should be apparent from them that both *Iliad* and *Odyssey* are coherent and carefully organized units. They also combine comprehensiveness with compactness in a remarkable way. For in both the whole period covered by the action extends over only a few weeks, while the events actually selected for narration occupy only about a dozen days.[18] Yet the *Iliad* is made to embrace by indirect reference both the beginning, long past, and the end, still to come, of the ten years war at Troy; and it expresses by example the essence of the war itself, its cruelty and vicissitudes, and the intensity of the experience of the men engaged. And the *Odyssey* is made to embrace all that has happened to Odysseus in the ten years since he started for home from Troy, and the fortunes too of the other Grecian heroes of the war—the 'homeward voyages' that are the theme of the household minstrel in the opening episode of the *Odyssey* itself– and the fates of those who fell.

The two stories moreover have each a subject that is of serious and universal human interest: in the one case, the temporary corruption of a noble nature, with awful consequences before its ultimate self-recovery; in the other, the reunion after long separation of man and wife, won by the endurance and the wisdom of them both.[19]

IMPERFECTIONS OF DETAIL AND THEIR CAUSES

The *Iliad* and the *Odyssey* bear each the imprint of a single creative mind. But we know from evidence internal to the poems themselves that their creator (or their respective creators as some prefer to think) inherited from predecessors in the practice of the art of poetry a poetic language, a method of composition involving the use of many recurrent phrases, a stock of such phrases already become traditional, and memories of a bygone age in which warriors fought with weapons of bronze and Mycenae and Pylos were rich and important seats of royal power.[20] It is a safe assumption that the inheritance included also a stock of stories and sequences or groups of stories associated with particular major themes, such as the war of the Greeks against Troy. We do not know to what extent our poet of *Iliad* or *Odyssey* may have incorporated bodily in his own composition whole episodes composed as such already by his predecessors; nor, if he did so, to what extent he preserved or modified his predecessors' language in repeating them; nor whether one or more of those predecessors bequeathed to him some earlier ventures in the organization of poems of substantial length on the basis of the relatively short pieces that must have been the normal unit of recitation. Nor do we know by what process either of the poems which we have was developed by its maker, or how many revisions by him it underwent before he left it. But we do know that throughout the period of time within which the *Iliad* and *Odyssey* were made the means of writing available, if they were available at all, were so cumbrous as to be no help for composition on this scale; so that the shaping and reshaping and improving of the poems must have been done by memory in the poet's head.[21] We do not know whether the finished product was also handed on by memory for some time before it was first committed to writing. But we do know that the texts of *Iliad* and *Odyssey* which we read—and which Cicero and Caesar and Horace and Virgil read before us—are younger by 350 years or more than the latest date conceivable for the creation of the works themselves. That during such a period of time some garbling of the original occurred is a matter more of certainty than of probability.[22]

When these facts are considered it is not surprising that some illogicalities and obscurities are observed in both *Iliad* and *Odyssey*; nor is it difficult to conjecture how these, in different ways, have arisen.

Thus, the catalogue of contingents in the second book of the *Iliad* is a feature whose general effect is so apt to the position it fills in the poem that Virgil and Milton both chose to imitate it, and it has left its mark on the mind of historians such as Herodotus and Thucydides as well. Yet it can hardly have been designed originally for the place in which it stands, since on inspection it is found to give a distribution of the various chieftains' dependencies that differs from that elsewhere assumed in the poem, it refers to ships in motion instead of to men marching on land, and it includes some leaders notoriously dead or absent at the time supposed—albeit it recognizes this anomaly in perfunctory postscripts.[23] Again, the episodes loosely assembled in the account of the first day's fighting are good in themselves, some very good indeed, and have a useful introductory relevance to the story that will follow. Yet they too can hardly have been designed originally for their present role, since some of them are really appropriate to the beginning of the war rather than to its tenth and final year (the supposed time of the *Iliad*'s action), and others are out of harmony with their immediate context. Priam will not really need by now to have his principal opponents identified for him by Helen; and cessation of general hostilities for a duel between Hector and Ajax will not be readily arranged a few hours after a similar duel between Menelaus and Paris has ended in a fiasco and been followed by the breaking of a solemn truce. Other incongruities seem to have arisen from other kinds of causes. When the embassy of conciliation to Achilles is proposed in the ninth book, Phoenix is to be included in the party, and later in fact plays an important and most moving part in · the proceedings: but in the account of the envoys' setting out and their arrival in Achilles' quarters he seems as the narrative stands to have been quite forgotten—which suggests, thought it does not prove, that an earlier version has been incompletely revised.[24] In the *Odyssey* the position of Ithaca in relation to the neighbouring islands has been either misunderstood by the narrator or garbled in later transmission,[25] as also probably has the point of the test by which Penelope lets Odysseus prove that he really is her long-awaited husband in the final scene of recognition.[26] And the visit of Odysseus to the

World of the Dead in the eleventh book appears from the curious manner of its insertion into the Circe-episode to be an afterthought.[27] If so, it is a considered afterthought well justified by its effect.

These are examples only, and many other oddities or incongruities of detail have been pointed out,[28,29] and others perhaps imagined, by scholarly investigation. That the poems include passages or modifications of passages composed originally for other contexts, and that they have been subjected to some garbling, and to some operations of afterthought, is as certain as can be; and also that there are traces in them of incomplete revision, or revisions, and that archaic features of composition still peer through their generally ingenious and calculated design. These facts have to be recognized and accepted, as they have been by appreciative readers for centuries past. They encourage the questing intellect to all manner of speculations. But the pursuit of these speculations, proper in itself and not wholly unfruitful, can lead away from the enjoyment of the excellence which both poems exhibit, in spite of all imperfections, in the versions which we have.

HOW THE STORIES ARE TOLD

In the *Iliad* and *Odyssey* the stories are presented partly in dramatic form, the poet's characters speaking in their own persons, and the element of pure narrative being reduced accordingly. This now familiar procedure was remarked by Aristotle (*Poetics* 24.14) as a peculiar merit of the *Iliad* and *Odyssey*, distinguishing them, in the extent of its employment, from all other poetic stories that he knew. In fact, about half of the total extent of the *Iliad* and *Odyssey* consists of direct speech of the participants. Seldom in either are there more than fifty continuous lines of uninterrupted narrative.

Thus even the *Iliad*'s predominantly narrative accounts of battle are diversified at intervals by the utterances of the fighting men, as they challenge or taunt their enemies, or concert action with friends, or shout encouragement or admonition; while in the *Odyssey* the predominantly narrative account of Odysseus' past adventures is punctuated here and there by his exchanges with giant or witch, or his instructions to his men, or (when he is alone on his way from Calypso's island to Phaeacia) by soliloquy. But more forcibly illustrative than this of the truth of Aristotle's remark is the fact that the personal tragedy of Achilles which makes the central theme of the *Iliad* is expressed essentially in four successive scenes of dramatic dialogue: the quarrel with Agamemnon, the rejection of Agamemnon's envoys' appeal, the scene with Thetis after Patroclus' death in which Achilles gives voice to his remorse and his new resolve, and the final scene in which Priam's entreaty wakes his sympathy and restores his humanity. And in the *Odyssey* the greater part of the story unfolds in conversations in domestic settings (Ithaca, Pylos, Sparta, Calypso's island, Phaeacia, and Ithaca again), in which the characters reveal their relations with one another and their reactions to the situation that has resulted from the long absence of Odysseus, and to the emergence of Telemachus into manhood, and to the appearance of the mysterious castaway who will turn out in the end to be Odysseus himself come home.

The dramatic form of presentation animates the stories throughout, because it interweaves with the movement of events a continuous and varied flow of human reactions to them: everything that happens elicits a positive response of human thought or feeling. Especially it intensifies passion and pathos, because terror and pity and grief are expressed directly by the people who experience them: the terror, for instance, of Hector's father and mother as they see him expose himself to certain death, and of his wife as she hears later the groans of the spectators on the wall; the pity of Achilles for Priam; the grief of the survivors of the war at Troy when the talk in Nestor's and Menalaus' houses turns their thoughts to the friends who did not survive. There are also two further particular reasons why the direct speech of the characters in the stories helps to reinforce the impression of their reality. First, because the impression of an extraordinary quality (the beauty of Helen, the magnificence of Menelaus' palace) can be imparted through the mouth of a third party, with the credibility that we attach by instinct to the spontaneous testimony of a witness present in time and place upon the scene: the measure of the remarkable is its effect on the beholder. Secondly, because our poet has the gift of reproducing an accent or manner or habit of speech that an experience of human behaviour which we share with him notes with a certain alacrity of recognition as permanently true to life: the manner of a mother comforting her child, of a woman welcoming a visitor at her door, of a young girl talking to an affectionate father, of an old nurse with her babies now grown up—'dear child' says Eurycleia to the forty-year-old Odysseus as he stands all bloodied among the corpses of the men he has killed. No less exactly recognizable is the crescendo of provocation and counter-provocation that raises the tempers in the quarrel scene that begins the *Iliad*; and the outpouring later of Achilles' long-brooded grievance, with its repetitions, and indignant questions, and insistent accumulated negatives.

This same appeal to experience which we share with the poet distinguishes the narrative as well as the dramatic element in both poems. The poet sees and hears in his imagination the story that he is telling. He sees and hears things and people at rest and in movement. He selects, whether by instinct or conscious purpose, the particulars that will help his hearers to see and hear, and feel, with him the reality of the story that is unfolding. The particulars which he thus selects are often very small, even trivial, in themselves: the hand that plucks a dress to attract attention, the wail of a frightened baby, the gentle disengagement of an embrace, the closing of a door-latch, the sound of a footstep, the glance that a person entering a room casts around in search of somewhere to sit. Of course the particulars chosen are usually less minute, and have often a very evidently distinctive character: an archer standing with bow full drawn, or a drunken giant slumped on his back with head askew. The foremost and commonest consequence of the choice is that it urgently but effortlessly invites us to see and hear with the poet.[30] But sometimes, indeed often, the detail chosen and offered us not only is readily seen or heard in the imagination, but also expresses or illustrates something additional to itself: the gentle movement with which Achilles disengages himself from Priam's suppliant hands is the visible expression of the change of his temper from hate to sympathy, the posture of the giant illustrates the fact of his drunken stupor. Finally, the chosen particular is often one that evokes a quick response from our own experience, so that across the 2,000 years and more that separate us in time we not only see and hear with the poet but enter directly as well into his feelings and those of the people in his story: we share with them our acquaintance with the behaviour of a frightened baby and the slow wagging of an old dog's tail in recognition of a friend, and when we surface from being under water we do just as Odysseus did after his submersion by the wave that swept him from his raft: 'at last he came up; and he spat away the salt water that streamed down from his head'.[31]

These characteristics of the poet's way of telling his story are important enough to invite documentation with some further instances.

Thus, lame Hephaestus stumping round the table as he serves the gods their wine, or Menelaus dragging Paris by the chin-strap of his helmet, or Ajax wielding his long pike as he strides from deck to deck of the line of ships, or Achilles standing with spear poised over the kneeling Lycaon, or Odysseus emerging naked from the bushes with a spray of foliage held before him, or Odysseus seated with bow drawn and arrow aimed for his dramatic shot through the axes—these all present easily imaginable postures to the mind's eye. And the crash with which the returning Cyclops dumps his load of faggots in the cave, or the clang of the bronze bowl in the silence of the hall when Eurycleia upsets it, or the twang of Odysseus' bowstring as he tests it before the hushed and wondering spectators—these all present easily imaginable sounds to the mind's ear, and do so moreover at dramatically exciting moments of the story. The long battle-scenes of the *Iliad* are full of precisely noted attitudes and movements and mutilations of the combatants, and their battle-cries and shouts and groans, and the ring or clatter of weapon on armour that accompanies the impact of spear or sword or arrow or hurled stone.

This effective but effortless appeal to the hearer's eye and ear is ubiquitous in both poems, and so also is its use in illustration. Achilles half-drawing his sword as his anger rises and slamming it home again in the scabbard as he regains his selfcontrol, Diomede thrusting his spear-point into the ground in sign of peace with the adversary whom he has recognized as a family friend, Hector as he recovers consciousness kneeling and vomiting and then fainting again, Telemachus snatching his hand from the hand of Antinous as he rejects his ingratiating approach, the Phaeacian herald leading the blind bard to his place in the hall and hanging his lyre on a peg and guiding his hand to find it, the Phaeacian spectators ducking as the quoit flies by—in these and similar cases the visual image evoked is in itself sharp and vivid, and in addition is expressive of something beyond itself: the state of mind of Achilles or Diomede or Telemachus, the fact of Hector's disablement or the bard's blindness or the impression made on the bystanders by the power of the quoit-cast. This illustrative or expressive effect of the particular chosen for mention is curiously exemplified in many references to facial expression—the scowls that attend often the opening of an angry speech, and the smiles or laughs that appear in a great variety of qualities, sometimes specified by the poet and sometimes left by him for his hearers' sympathy to supply from the context: smiles grateful, conciliatory, affectionate, grimly confident, amused, ambiguous, satisfied, cruel, indulgent, approving, knowing, contemptuous, and laughs tearful, forced, vague, hysterical, tense, giggling, gleeful, and so on.[32]

When Hector enters Troy on a mission from the battlefield, the women crowd around him in the street with eager questions about the safety of their sons and husbands. When on his way back to the battlefield he and his wife are for a little while together, they find a momentary relief from the tension of parting in shared amusement at their little son's fear of his father's helmet. When Telemachus greets his visitor at the beginning of the *Odyssey* he takes his spear from him and puts it in the spear-stand which still holds the spears Odysseus left when he went to Troy, visible daily reminders of their absent owner. When Odysseus towards the end of the story gets the deadly bow into his hands, he turns it this way and that as he inspects it at leisure, watched by the suitors with attentive curiosity and expectation. The feelings evoked in these situations are instantly and vividly recognizable to us from our own experience in other contexts; we share them with the poet and the people in the story. This is true also of the feeling we associate with being wakened by voices, as Odysseus is by the cry of Nausicaa's maids; or with the sound of voices heard passing in the quiet of night, before sleep comes, as Odysseus on the night before the crisis hears the chatter of the maidservants going out to join their lovers; or with sounds heard while their source is still mysterious or at least unseen, like the bleating of the Cyclops' sheep heard across the strait, or Circe singing inside her house, or the lowing of the fatal cattle that Odysseus and his men hear as his ship approaches the island of the sun-god, or the sound of the lyre within that Odysseus hears as he stands outside his own house, come home after twenty years. In the same way we are invited to enter directly into the feelings of Achilles, as he looks out over the plain and sees from the turn the battle is taking that something disastrous has happened, and fears but does not yet know that this is Patroclus' death; or with the feelings of Andromache, busy with her loom at home, when she hears the groan go up from the Trojans on the wall.

CHARACTERIZATION

The people in the poems are made as real as the events, and with the same clarity and economy of effort. The poet sees them in the way in which we see people—other than our intimates—in our own daily life, distinguishing them as individuals in our minds by a few (but only a few) identifying characteristics. These may include qualities of moral disposition (courage, amiability, honesty, etc.) and style (taciturnity, garrulity, etc.), but also physical mannerisms (peering, stuttering, etc.), and physical characteristics (stature, hair-colour, corpulence or skinniness, etc.); and also any of a variety of other facts about a person, such as role (nurse, parson, porter, etc.) or condition (old age, sickness, bereavement) or distinctive past experience (survivor of a disaster, maker of a discovery, etc.) or accomplishment (musician, athlete, wit, etc.)—or many other things.

The characterization of the people in a story is not necessarily concerned with the study of 'character' in the usual sense of the term: it is a matter of identifying 'characteristics' which may be of many different kinds. The number of such characteristics that we are positively aware of depends on the nearness of our acquaintance and the degree of our attention.

The ways in which we become aware of such characteristics are various also. But when intimate acquaintance is excluded they reduce themselves effectively to four: habitual behaviour of the person in question, behaviour on a particular occasion that leaves a lasting impression, the known reactions or judgements of others, and, sometimes, physical or biographical attributes of a sufficiently distinctive kind. Impressions thus formed may be sharpened and emphasized by an awareness of a contrast with some other person who invites comparison in virtue of some one characteristic held in common—a brother for instance, or a predecessor in office, or a rival in a competition.

It is in these ways that the poet of *Iliad* or *Odyssey* sees his people as individually distinct and makes us aware of their individuality. Because they are many and various, and seen in various ways, the result is animation; because they are seen in ways familiar to us, the result is a sense of reality.

Among the secondary characters of the *Iliad* are two, Nestor and Odysseus, who are distinguished by mental abilities as well as physical prowess. Nestor is a very old man, though hale and active. He has a pronounced mannerism supposedly associated with old age, a fondness for long-winded reminiscence. He has tact, and is adept at easing the tension in difficult situations; for which purpose he makes adroit use of his own long-windedness. He is an artful diplomatist, seeing and seizing on the right moment, when it offers, to make the suggestion that will gain his end. All this we know from repeated illustrations in the course of the story. It is all that we do know, that is significant, but it suffices to make Nestor a live and real individual.[33] Odysseus too is a man of thought as well as action, but in a somewhat different style, and the contrast with that of Nestor helps to sharpen our awareness of the distinctive qualities of both. He is a younger man than Nestor, and typically chosen for active missions of a diplomatic nature. He is a persuasive speaker. He is also a straight thinker, and a cool head. All this we learn from repeated illustration or report in the course of the story. We also learn from one highly distinctive scene that he is a man of quick and decisive action, and from one highly distinctive soliloquy that his courage is not of the kind that knows no fear but of the kind that knows fear and overcomes it.[34]

Agamemnon and Menelaus are brothers; Agamemnon the elder, and leader of the expedition, though it is for Menelaus' sake that it has been undertaken. Menelaus is less well endowed with physical strength and skill than the other Greek princes who are his peers. He knows his own limitations, but does his best within them. He is willing and persevering, and he recognizes his duty to those who are fighting for his sake. All this appears from a few strongly significant scenes, and from his ubiquitous persistent endeavour throughout the fighting.[35] His merits are emphasized by the contrast between him and his rival Alexandros (Paris), who appears in more scenes than one as selfish and self-indulgent, cause of his people's troubles but careless of his responsibility. There is a contrast also between Menelaus and Agamemnon, who has an impressive physical endowment to match his superiority of power and position, but a poor spirit, irresolute and easily discouraged. Agamemnon is also overbearing and avaricious. All this is made plain by repeated illustration, in his speech and behaviour and comment of others.[36]

The two most prominent fighters among the Greeks after Achilles' withdrawal are Diomede and Ajax. Diomede dominates the first day's battle, fighting with a frenzied fury inspired by Athena. After the reverse suffered by the Greeks on the second and third day, when Diomede is wounded and disabled, it is Ajax who is the mainstay of the defence. Diomede is aggressive in action, and terse and decided in speech. He knows clearly what are his duties and what are his rights, and insists on both.[37] Ajax speaks very little, though he speaks sensibly when he does. He is strongest of the Greeks after Achilles. He is big and burly. He carries a large and massive shield, often mentioned as a distinctive attribute, and symbolizing in effect his character as a bulwark of defence. Repeatedly Ajax is called to help when things are difficult. Repeatedly he is seen defending a threatened position, or covering a retreat. In style and role he stands in evident contrast to Diomede, with whom as his counterpart in the first day's fighting he invites comparison.[38]

The personalities of the gods in the *Iliad* become apparent in the same ways as do those of the humans: through significant moments of behaviour, single or repeated, and through the comments of others in the story. Thus, Hera is chronically at odds with her husband Zeus, though also afraid of him. She and Athena are both remorselessly vindictive in pursuit of their private grudge against the Trojans, and consequently resentful of Zeus' plan to help the Greeks. But Athena only once lets her resentment find expression. She is prudent and ingenious and unscrupulous. She favours the sensible soldier Diomede and the cool calculator Odysseus; and she easily overthrows her fellow-Olympian Ares, the blustering but stupid and clumsy god who *likes* fighting. Hephaestus is sufficiently individualized as the god who is a cripple and an artisan; Thetis, as the grieving mother of a son doomed soon to die. Zeus is held in awe by all the gods, on whom he enforces his will by reminders of past demonstrations of brute force: he is far stronger than all of them together. But he is subject to petty vexations, and sorrows, and regrets; and he can pity the mortals whose sufferings he observes.[39]

In the *Odyssey*, where the context is different, Zeus appears in a different light from that in which the *Iliad* displays him. He is secure and relaxed in his supremacy among the gods, and benevolent in the exercise of it—gladly authorizing as deserved the safe homecoming of Odysseus and punishment of the suitors' murderous design, and soothing the ruffled dignity of Poseidon when Poseidon learns that the hero has been saved by the Phaeacians from further persecution by him. Zeus, Poseidon, and Athena are the only major divinities who have active importance in the *Odyssey*. Athena, superintending the development of the story, makes very frequent appearances, but commonly in disguise, and so not in her own character. Two scenes however are agreeably expressive of her distinctive style: when she takes adroit advantage of Poseidon's absence, and the opportunity offered by a chance remark of Zeus', to raise among the gods the delicate subject of the hero's homecoming, which Poseidon has been persistently opposing: and when, after some sparring in mendacity between her protégé and herself, she approves his artfulness with an affectionate smile and declares that it is this that endears him to her.[40]

Of the human participants in the *Odyssey* the suitors Antinoüs and

Eurymachus are among the most prominent. Repeated illustrations in act and speech show that Antinoüs is assertive and brutal, Eurymachus cunning and treacherous. Antinoüs takes the lead for the sake of taking it; Eurymachus is content to let him, except when there is advantage to be gained from acting or speaking first. Eurymachus has also ingratiated himself with two of the servants in Odysseus' household. From the remarks of others we learn that he, not the ringleader Antinoüs, is regarded as the suitor whose suit is most likely to succeed.[41]

The old nurse Eurycleia in the *Odyssey* is a secondary character drawn on about the same scale as the leading suitors. But the distinctive fact felt in her case is not personal 'character' but role—her occupation and her position in the household. She has nursed Odysseus and Telemachus successively as babies, she is an old woman, is devoted to the family, and now is housekeeper and confidential attendant of Penelope. As such she appears in successive scenes engaged in domestic activities typical and expressive of her position; lighting the young master to bed, arranging the furniture, directing the household duties of the maids. Her status in the household is reflected too in the tone and manner of address used by her to members of the family and by them to her.[42]

The characterization of the swineherd Eumaeus is essentially of the same kind, governed by his occupation and relationship with Odysseus' family: these are illustrated repeatedly in his behaviour and sentiments and in the style of speech used by him and towards him, and also of course by the setting in which he first appears. But as the development of the story involves a long period of leisurely conversation and social activity while he is entertaining the disguised Odysseus in his hut, we become aware of a number of qualities personal to him which are separable from, though complementary to, those attaching to the type that he represents; we find from his acts and words that he is kind-hearted, discreet, efficient, enterprising, pious, conscientious, and so on; and finally we hear the story of his past experience which is both memorable and wholly individual to himself.[43]

In the characterization of Penelope and Telemachus the poet is primarily concerned with their behaviour in a personal situation. Penelope is a clever woman and a wife with a strong attachment to her husband. Telemachus is a well-bred young man just growing up. Neither condition is markedly distinctive in itself, though both can be, and are, illustrated in an interesting way. But their situations are very distinctive indeed. Penelope's husband has been long absent; her hopes of his return are far-faded though not quite extinct; she has for long been under strong pressure to remarry; now the exhaustion of her expedients for delay and the emergence of her son into manhood combine to urge her to a decision, while at the same time she is tantalized by hope-raising reports of a kind which alas have repeatedly disappointed her in the past. It is a further complication that her own husband, come home in disguise, dare not reveal himself to her until he has disposed of the enemies who infest her house in greatly superior force. Against this background it has to be contrived that she should surrender (or appear to surrender) to the suitors' importunity with her unrecognized husband's encouragement but without compromising her long-sustained loyalty to him—from which it results that her behaviour as the dénouement approaches is enigmatic. And it has also to be contrived that she should joyfully recognize him after he has concealed his identity from her—a problem which the poet solves with conspicuous success, though not without invoking for a moment the aid of the supernatural.

Telemachus' emergence into manhood brings about a confrontation with the suitors and an abrupt change in his relationship with his mother. To them he is now a menace; to her he is a cherished object of solicitude, but also, suddenly, the man of the house, and as such something of a surprise. He is also the beloved young master to the old servants of the family; and an erstwhile comrade's son, a well-mannered and attractive young fellow (so like his father, too), to the grand friends of Odysseus whom he visits on his travels; and a natural dispenser of hospitality and protection to the fugitive nobleman Theoclymenus and the destitute vagabond (his own father disguised and as yet unrecognized) who seek shelter in his house. To all these he behaves (and they behave to him) in a way that corresponds to his age, and social position and personal relationship with them.[44]

With Hector in the *Iliad* what individualizes him is again different: it is not primarily a matter of personal characteristics, nor of reaction to a given set of circumstances—though in fact elements of all of these are emphasized and contribute to the total effect: what leaves us with our strongest impression about Hector is his experience, what happens to him in the story. It is a tragic experience in the classic sense of the term: leader of his people in a war for survival against a foreign invader, he enjoys an unexpected victory over greatly superior forces, and comes within an inch of a further victory which would be decisive. Then his luck turns against him. Over-confident from his previous success, and unwilling to abandon the hope it gave him, he rejects wiser counsels and insists on keeping his army in the field.

As a result they are defeated with great slaughter. Remorseful and ashamed, he engages in single combat with an adversary for whom he knows he is no match, and is killed. The gods, who could or would not save him from his fate, honour him with concern for the proper burial of his body. His fellow-citizens honour his memory with gratitude for his patriotism and praise for his kindness and courage. The pathos of Hector's experience is enhanced by the fact that we know, but he does not, that his success was destined never to be anything but temporary, and is engineered by the king of the gods simply as a means of giving Achilles the revenge on Agamemnon for which he has prayed. It is enhanced further by the fact (brought out in three successive illustrations) that in physical strength and skill he is not normally superior even to the second order of fighting men on the Greek side; and by a memorable scene with his wife and baby son which fixes in our minds the cause for which he is fighting and makes us feel for him throughout the story as typically human as well as heroic.[45]

Of the principal figures in the two epics, Achilles and Odysseus, the latter is characterized in fairly simple terms; his two dominant qualities, resource and endurance, were evidently given in the tradition and are necessarily illustrated with persistence in the story of his adventures in his wanderings and in the situation he finds at home. There is indeed some slight awkwardness apparent in harmonizing the hero of fairytale (the man who tricks the Cyclops by giving No-man as his name) with the real person that Odysseus has become in the story as a whole, but this after all is not often felt. Apart from sagacity and endurance the qualities of Odysseus that appear in the story are two. First, the capacity to inspire affection and regard as husband, man and king (illustrated by the attitude of Penelope and Calypso and the Phaeacians, and the way in which he is spoken of by Eumaeus and his supporters in Ithaca, and by Nestor, Helen and Menelaus); secondly a degree of strength and skill (expressed in three illustrative feats—his casual but triumphant quoit-cast at the Phaeacian games, the 'gentle tap' that renders his opponent unconscious in the fight with the bully Irus, and the effortless stringing of the bow in the dénouement after all the rest have failed) that separates him from the ordinary people in the story and makes him the only person in it to compare in magnitude with the heroic figures of the *Iliad*. In essence, the person of Odysseus in the *Odyssey* is rendered in the same way as are the secondary figures in the *Iliad*, though with more emphasis and in a great variety of interesting and exciting situations, by the expression of a few constant attributes, and by the contrast with others that makes his personal magnitude apparent. But he has a significance that extends beyond his person, as the man longing and longed for, who has rejected even immortality for the love of home.[46]

The characterization of Achilles is more complicated, and developed in a way that is not elsewhere exemplified in either of the poems. He is distinguished to begin with by one purely physical but most emphatic attribute, an incomparable endowment of manly beauty, strength and skill and courage. With this are combined four distinctive qualities of a moral order, qualities of character in the special sense of the word. First is a fundamental humanity and nobleness of nature, obscured indeed throughout much of the story by disturbed emotion, but apparent in moments of behaviour, implied by the regard and affection of worthy friends, and affirmed in the closing scenes by the testimony of Zeus and by Achilles' own conduct. Second is a fierce and unruly temper. Third is an intense preoccupation with what he sees as his honour. Fourth is his feeling for his father Peleus, of whom from time to time we are reminded; whose spear he wields (16.143), whose arms he wears (17.194), whose horses he drives (17.443), and who sent with him to the war his old counsellor Phoenix (9.438) and the squire and friend Patroclus whom he loves (23.90). In the story given us his sensitivity in regard to his honour, working on his choleric temper, generates in two stages of ascending intensity a pathological hatred that corrupts his sense of honour itself and leads him to act in a manner that excites disgust, first among his friends and then even among the gods. This is resolved in the end by an appeal to another emotion, his feeling for his absent father; and this restores him to his normal self, but deprived now by his own act of his dearest friend, and himself doomed by his own choice to an early death.

Thus in the characterization of Achilles are involved several attributes of the inner self; and these are not only exhibited, but exhibited in interaction one with another in the course of a developing experience of the inner self which between them they generate. Moreover that experience in its successive phases interacts with external events, in turn affecting and being affected by them, so that the character of Achilles is the mainspring of the whole action of the *Iliad*.

The thought of Achilles' own death, present in the background from the beginning of the story, becomes insistent from the moment when he sets out to avenge Patroclus. 'For after Hector's death your own must quickly follow', says his mother sadly when he declares his resolve. The prophecy is repeated in other terms by the miraculous utterance of the horse Xanthus, by the dying Hector, by Patroclus' ghost, and by his mother again when she brings him Zeus' command to allow the ransoming of Hector's body. It is symbolically confirmed by his offering on Patroclus' pyre of the lock of his own hair which his father had promised to the river-god in his homeland when praying for his safe return.

A cluster of affectionate and pathetic figures surround Achilles: his father, old and unprotected, far away, and fated never to see his only son again; his mother, knowing and dreading his imminent death, and doing to please him things that she knows must hasten it; old Phoenix, doomed by a curse to have no son of his own, who has given him a father's love since babyhood; and Patroclus, 'kind to all', victim of his own kindness and his friend's blind passion, whose last prayer is to be buried with him so that they may be together in death as they were in life.[47]

ILLUSTRATIVE EXAMPLES IN TRANSLATION

The passages in translation which now follow may help to illustrate some of what has been said above: in particular, how narrative co-operates with dialogue and vice versa; and how concentration on often quite small details of behaviour or appearance (familiar but not too obviously familiar from experience shared by his hearers or readers with the poet) can impart of their own accord a conviction of reality, and sometimes also excite a response of feeling—so that we both see and feel the story that is being told. It will be observed also how a scene animated by these means can communicate an aspect of a character or the emotional content of a situation with little or no direct suggestion of this by the poet. The passages to be given here as examples do in fact all occur at points where the management of emotional tone is important to the aesthetic effect of the stories taken as wholes.

Iliad 6. 392–502

Hector has returned briefly to the town of Troy during the first day's inconclusive fighting. His mission completed, he is now on his way back to the battlefield. His brilliant but temporary successes are still to come. We see him here with his wife and child for the last time before his death at the hands of Achilles, which is to follow two days later.

The pathos of the dialogue between husband and wife, and the dramatic irony implicit in Hector's prayer, require no comment. What may invite comment is the extremely economical yet expressive use of the narrative element, focussed on a few minutely perceived details. Hector's smile at the sight of his little son, the child's fright, the laugh shared by his father and mother, the dandling, the smile on the mother's tearful face, the husband's brief affectionate gesture—all these are in themselves easily imaginable to the mind's eye, and also instantly recognizable from simple experience shared with the poet by people of all times and places since. Especially evocative is the shared laugh which interrupts for a moment the painful tension of the parting. The scene is not only moving in itself: it fixes in the mind one aspect of Hector's role in the story, as defender of home and family, and so contributes essentially to the perspective in which his personal tragedy is seen, and by which also our sympathies between Greeks and Trojans are held in balance.

As he went on his way through the wide city and came to the Scaean gate, by which he was to go out on to the plain to the battlefield, there he met his wife, hurrying towards him, his bride of many gifts, Andromache daughter of great-hearted Eëtion, Eëtion whose home was beneath the wooded hill of Placus, in Thebe under Placus, and he was king of the men of Cilicia: his daughter it was whom bronze-helmed Hector had to wife, and now she came to meet him and with her a serving-woman carried their child on her bosom, an infant still, a little baby, Hector's much-loved son, beautiful as a bright star, whom Hector called Scamandrius but most called Astyanax, because Hector alone saved Ilium from destruction. Hector as he looked at his son smiled and was silent. And Andromache came and stood by him, weeping tears, and laid her hand on his arm and spoke to him, saying: 'Alas, dear husband, your courage will be the death of you. You have no pity for your little son nor for me your poor wife. Soon I shall be a widow; for soon the Achaeans will set on you all together and kill you. But if you are taken from me I should be better dead and buried; there can be no other comfort for me once you have met your doom. I have no father now, nor lady mother; for the lord Achilles killed my father, and sacked the strong city of the Cilicians, high-gated Thebe. He killed Eëtion, but he had respect for him, and did not spoil him of his armour, but burned his body with all his brave panoply, and heaped a mound over the grave; and the mountain-nymphs planted elm-trees around it, the daughters of Zeus who wields the aegis. And the seven brothers that I had, that were with me in our home—they all went on one day together to the house of Hades, all slain by the lord Achilles fleet of foot as they fought to save our shambling oxen and our white-fleeced sheep. And my mother, who was Queen under wooded Placus—her Achilles brought hither with the rest of our possessions; and then for a great price paid he set her free again, but the archer-goddess Artemis struck her down in her own father's house. O Hector, you are father and lady mother to me, and brother too, and you are my brave strong husband. Come, have pity on me. Stay here by the wall; do not make your son an orphan and your wife a widow. And have men stand fast by the wild-fig tree, where the ascent to the city is easiest and the way most open to storm the wall. Three times already the enemy's best men have made attempts there, the two Ajaxes and famed Idomeneus and Tydeus' warrior son, and those they lead; some seer and prophet has given them the word perhaps, or it may be their own valour prompts them and sets them on.'

Great Hector of the glittering helmet answered her: 'I too am mindful, wife, of all these things. But I dread the shame that I must feel before the Trojans and the Trojan women with their trailing gowns, if like a weakling I hang back from the battle. Nor does my own heart prompt me otherwise, for I have taught myself to be a brave soldier always and to fight among the fore-most of my people, winning high honour for my father and myself. For this I well know in my own heart and my own mind: the day must come when the strong town of Ilium will fall, and Priam and the people of Priam, famed wielder of the ashen spear. But I do not grieve so much for the suffering of the Trojans in time to come, nor for Hecuba herself, nor for king Priam, nor for my brothers, my many brave brothers who must fall in the dust by the hand of our enemy—so much as I grieve for you, to think of you led away weeping by some bronze-mailed Achaean, the day of freedom taken from you, to work a loom perhaps in Argos at another woman's orders, and fetch water from Messeis or Hypereia, all unwilling, under merciless constraint; and some man may say as he sees you weeping "this woman was wife to Hector, bravest of all the Trojans, tamers of horses, in those days when men fought before Ilium"—so will some man say, and more misery will be added to your misery, for the want of a husband able as I am to stand between you and the day of slavery. But may I be dead and the earth heaped upon my grave, sooner than I should hear your cries and know that you are dragged away a prisoner.' So Hector spoke, and reached out to take his child into his arms. But the baby shrank back with a wail to the bosom of the trim-girdled nurse, in fear at the sight of his own father, frightened by the bronze and the horsehair crest as he saw it nod menacingly from the helmet peak. At this they laughed, his loving father and his lady mother; and Hector took the helmet from his head and set it down, all shining, on the ground. He kissed his child and dandled him; and then he prayed to Zeus and all the gods, saying: 'Zeus and all gods that are, grant that this my son may be renowned among the Trojans even as I am, and as strong and as valiant, and may he rule with power in Ilium, and in time to come may they say "Here is one who is a better man by far than his father", as he comes home from war bearing the bloodstained armour of an enemy he has slain, and may he make his mother proud.'

So Hector spoke, and gave the child into his dear wife's arms, and she took him and held him to her perfumed breast, still smiling through her tears. And her husband saw and pitied her, and he fondled her, and spoke saying: 'Dear heart, do not grieve so much; for no man shall send me down to Hades before my fated time; and no mortal born can escape what is fated, be he coward or be he brave—of that you may be sure. Now go home, and attend to your own work with loom and distaff, and bid your servants go about their tasks. But war must be men's business, and mine especially of all the men that are in Ilium.'

So saying brave Hector took up again his helmet with its horse-hair crest; and his dear wife went away homeward, often turning back, weeping great tears; and soon she came to the lordly house of manslaying Hector, and found many of her women waiting there, and set them all aweeping. They wept for Hector in his house while he was still alive; for they did not believe that he would ever come home again from the battle, escaping the fury and might of the Achaeans.

Iliad 8. 553–565

The Trojans have overwhelmed the Greeks in the second day's fighting and have driven them back into their camp. They themselves now bivouac on the battlefield, full of bright hopes for a decisive victory when battle is resumed next day. This is a turning-point in their fortunes. Two pictures are offered to the mind's eye—a brilliant star-spangled sky, and the half-lit figures of men gathered around their camp-fires. The responses of feeling which these excite in the poet's audience are transferred by him to the participants in his story, and particularized as exhilaration and expectancy.

> But they with high hearts camped all night long upon the field of battle; and they kindled many watch-fires. As when the stars and shining moon in the heavens are bright to see, when all on high is still and the sky is clear, and every peak and headland and valley is revealed, and the boundless firmament is rent wide open, and all the stars shine out, and a shepherd's heart is glad—so many then between the ships and the stream of Xanthus were the watch-fires of the Trojans that blazed before Ilium town. A thousand fires were burning on the plain, and at each sat fifty men in the glare of the flames. And the horses, champing millet and white barley, stood by the chariots waiting for bright-throned Dawn.

Iliad 18. 369–427

Achilles has been moved to bitter grief and rage by the death of Patroclus, which shortly he will set out in fury to avenge. But his armour has been lost with Patroclus, to whom he had lent it. His mother Thetis now goes to ask the smith-god Hephaestus to make him new equipment.

This gives occasion for an interlude deliberately contrasted in tone with the passions that precede and follow it. The smith is in his workshop. His wife welcomes the visitor at the door, and calls her husband in to hear what he can do for her. A touch of humour attaches to the realism of these mundane proceedings, in that smith and wife and visitor are gods. The products of Hephaestus' craft are supernatural, but his activity and behaviour are those of a very human artisan, and are matched by the tone of his wife's words to Thetis and to him. The cleaning up of his person before he goes in to greet his visitor is nicely observed, as also is his workmanlike tidiness about his tools.

His physique, so expressive both of his lameness and of his occupation, is made very vividly visible. As a genre piece the scene is engaging in itself. But it is also designedly functional for the variation of tone that it introduces at this point of the story.

Meanwhile the silver-footed goddess Thetis came to Hephaestus' house, the house of bronze, eternal, star-illumined, a marvel even among the immortals, which the cripple god had built for himself with his own hands. She found him busy about his bellows, perspiring as he turned in his hurry this way and that. He was making a set of twenty great bowls on tripod feet, to stand in his stately hall along the walls; and he had put golden wheels beneath their bases, on which they should come and go of their own accord to the gatherings of the gods—a wonder to behold. They were almost finished: only the handles, of curious workmanship, were still to be added; and these he was fixing, hammering the rivets. While he was busy thus about his craft, the silver-footed goddess Thetis drew near to the house. And Charis came out to the gate and saw her, the bright-veiled Grace who was wife to the crippled god, that famous craftsman. She took Thetis by the hand, and greeted her by name, and said: 'What brings you to our house, dear honoured friend? You have not often been our way before. Come in, and let me welcome you with some refreshment.' So saying the lovely goddess led the way indoors, and had Thetis sit down on a chair with silver trimmings and a stool before it to rest the feet on. And she called to Hephaestus: 'Come into the house, Hephaestus. Thetis is here, and has something to ask of you.' And the cripple god, the famous craftsman, answered saying: 'Why, this is a goddess whom I much revere and honour that is come to visit us. It is she who saved me when I had my great fall, through my heartless mother's wilful doing, who wanted to hide me from sight, because I was lame. Grievous then indeed would my plight have been, had not Eurynome and Thetis caught me in their arms, Eurynome daughter of Ocean that flows full circle. With them I lived nine years and made many a piece of delicate metal-work: brooches, and bracelets and petalled pins and necklaces—there in the hollow cave, and all around the stream of Ocean flowed foaming and murmuring without pause or end; and no one knew it, god or man, but Thetis only and Eurynome who had saved me. She, my preserver, it is who has come now to our house, and so I must pay in full the debt I owe to fair-tressed Thetis for my rescue. But do you set fit entertainment before her, while I put away my bellows and the rest of my tools.' This said, he stood up from his anvil, a giant in bulk on shrunken legs that went with halting steps. He took his bellows from the fire and set them aside, and he gathered together the tools he worked with and stowed them in a silver chest. And he sponged his face and brawny neck and hairy chest, and put on his tunic, and took a stout stick and made his way limping to the door. Supporting him on either side walked two attendants made of gold in the likeness of living girls: they can think and speak and move and the gods have given them sundry skills. These were attentive to him, and he leaned on them. He limped over to where Thetis was, and sat down beside her on a polished chair, and took her hand, and greeted her by name, and said: 'Why, dear and honoured friend, are you come to our house? Tell me your purpose, and with all my heart I will do what you desire, if I am able, and if done it can be.'

Odyssey 1. 425–444

Telemachus has been roused by his visitor (the pretended merchant-man who is really the goddess Athena) to give warning to the suitors to quit his house. He has just told them that he will summon an assembly of the Ithacans next day, to proclaim the warning before witnesses. He intends also to carry out the second part of his visitor's advice, to make a journey to the mainland in quest of news of his father. Thus he is now asserting himself for the first time as a grown man and head of the household. Eurycleia, whose solicitous attendance on her young master is here described, has nursed Odysseus too when he was little; and it is she who will recognize Odysseus later by the scar he got boar-hunting in his youth, and so come near to betraying his disguise.

The minutely particularized narrative which here follows serves to characterize Eurycleia at once, and firmly, in her role in the household and her relationship with Telemachus. It also helps to make the household and its everyday domestic routine a concrete reality to the imagination. There will be several other little scenes of similar effect as the story proceeds. But this one has a separate and more important effect; which is to mark a notable moment in the experience of Telemachus, into whose feelings we are invited to enter. When his old nurse has completed her attentions and goes out, the curious emphasis laid on the closing of the door after her and the movement of its bolt, as it is drawn by a hand now invisible to him, expresses the fact that he is now—and feels that he is—alone with his thoughts. These thoughts, mentioned already at the beginning of the passage, are of dangers and adventures that loom ahead; and the protective warmth of the bed-clothes under which he lies make a piquant contrast with them. So also do the protective attentions of Eurycleia, now withdrawn. The details have been chosen with a quite subtle instinct for their significance.

And Telemachus went to bed where he had his own chamber, opening on the elegant courtyard . . . and his thoughts as he went were busy with many matters. With him, carrying a burning pine-torch, went faithful Eurycleia, daughter of Ops, Peisenor's son. Laertes had bought her for a price long years before when she was young, paying the value of twenty oxen; and he honoured her in the household no less than he did his own true wife, but never lay with her, fearing his wife's displeasure. She it was who now went with Telemachus, carrying the burning torch; and she loved him dearly, more than did any of the other serving-women, and had been his nurse when he was little. Telemachus opened the door of the well-built chamber, and went and sat down on the bed, and took off his soft tunic, and handed it to the careful old woman. She folded it and smoothed it and hung it up on a peg beside the morticed bedstead; and then she went out of the room, pulling the door to by its silver handle and drawing the bolt by its thong. And there Telemachus lay, snug under a fleece of wool, and thought all night long about the journey which Athene had told him he must undertake.

Odyssey 17. 260-334

Much changed in appearance and disguised as a ragged castaway, Odysseus has been hospitably received, but not recognized, by the swineherd Eumaeus. The two have just come from Eumaeus' hut, and now stand in front of Odysseus' house in the town of Ithaca, where Odysseus proposes to observe the suitors while he acts the part of a beggar. It is the first time that he has seen his home for twenty years; and as we know, it has fallen meanwhile on evil days. Odysseus must avoid recognition, or he will be in danger from the suitors, who are numerous and unprincipled.

This is an extraordinary moment and one that must stir strong and manifold emotions in the hero. The poet does not attempt to describe these, but makes us aware of them through our instinctive reaction to the facts that he narrates. Everyone is familiar with the quickening of sensibility that is aroused by sounds off stage, as it were—by information received from the ear before the eye can disclose its origin and significance. And so everyone can enter, to this extent, into the feelings of Odysseus as he hears the sound of music from inside the house before which he stands and which he is about to enter, for the first time in twenty years. But of course there is much more beside this that is moving in his situation: the irony of the manner of his homecoming, the danger of premature recognition, the pathos of the forlorn condition of his home and friends. Much of this is indicated, explicitly or by implication, in the dialogue between Odysseus and his companion. But it finds its most forcible, though oblique, expression in the brief encounter of the hero with the superannuated and neglected dog, who alone recognizes him, whose recognition might betray him, whose condition is symbolic of the fallen state of the household, and whose loyalty and distress are acknowledged by Odysseus with a momentary tear that he dare not let be seen. This encounter is described in terms of a short statement of fact and a series of very slight but significant movements that common experience makes us quick to recognize. As the dog lies, vermin-infested, amid the dung, he lifts his head and pricks up his ears—this is attention; he droops his ears and wags his tail—this is recognition and welcome; and Odysseus turns away and brushes a tear from his eye—this is suppressed emotion. Eumaeus in reply to a question refers to the dog's prowess in earlier days with the effect (unintended by Eumaeus) of an epitaph, and points to his neglected state as an illustration of what comes to pass in a household that has no master. Then he goes into the house, and the dog dies—having seen his master again, as the poet remarks, after nineteen years. The remark is objectively offered, and any sentiment attaching to it is supplied by the reader, not forced upon him by the poet.

It will be noticed that the setting of the episode, outside Odysseus' house, is made visible without direct description by having Odysseus comment to his companion on the impression it makes on him as a stranger supposedly unacquainted with it. It is worth noticing also that as Odysseus turns to Eumaeus with this observation, he touches him on the arm (or hand). The mention of this trivial but familiar gesture activates the mind's eye; and so later does the glance that Eumaeus casts around for something to sit on, at the moment of his entry into the hall.

And now Odysseus and the worthy swineherd arrived, and stopped outside the house. The sound of the hollow lyre came to their ears, for Phemius was striking up, about to begin a song. Odysseus touched the swineherd on the arm, and said: 'Eumaeus, surely this fine house must be the house of Odysseus. It is easy to know it for what it is, even among many; for there are several buildings joined to one another, and the courtyard is walled, and its wall has a coping, and these are good strong double doors; surely no one could do otherwise than admire it. And I can tell that there are many men feasting inside the house, for there is a smell of roast in the air, and the music of a lyre too, which the gods have made to be companion of feasting.' The swineherd Eumaeus answered him and said: 'You have been quick to recognize the house; and indeed you always have your wits about you. But come now, let us think how we are to proceed. Either do you go first into the lordly house and enter among the wooers, and I will wait behind you here outside; or, if you will, do you wait here, and I will go in first. But do not linger here too long, or someone may notice you before you get inside and you may be pelted or be knocked about. Remember that, I beg you, and take care.' Then much-enduring brave Odysseus answered him: 'I follow you; I take your purpose; your warning is well understood. But do you enter first, and I will wait behind out here. For I have had long experience of buffetings and peltings, and my heart is not easily daunted after many sufferings amid waves and war: let this new trial be one more after many. The belly's craving cannot be suppressed: a cruel curse it is, cause of much misery to human kind . . .'

While thus they were talking together a dog who was lying there lifted his head and pricked up his ears—Argus, brave-hearted Odysseus' dog, whom long ago he had reared for his own, but had no profit of him, for before that could be he went away to war against the strong town of Troy. This dog the young men used in the past to take with them when they went hunting wild goats and deer and hares. But now he lay neglected—for his master was gone—amid the dung that was piled in plenty outside the gate, droppings of mules and oxen, ready for the servants to cart away to dung the broad fields of Odysseus' royal domain. There lay the dog Argus, covered with dog-ticks. At once he knew that Odysseus was at hand, and he slowly wagged his tail and let his ears drop back, but he had not the strength to come nearer to his master. Then Odysseus turned his face away, and brushed a tear from his eye, unnoticed by Eumaeus. And he made haste to question the swineherd, saying: 'Eumaeus, here is a strange sight, this dog lying in the dung. He seems a fine creature; but I wonder if he had speed in his day to match these looks; or was he just a dog of the kind that hang about men's tables, and their masters feed and cosset them for show?' The swineherd Eumaeus answered him and said: 'This truly is the dog of a man dead far away. If he had now the beauty and the strength that he had when Odysseus went to Troy and left him, then indeed you would wonder, to see his speed and spirit. No quarry could escape him, even in the depths of the forest; for he excelled in tracking too. But now he is in a sorry state, and his master has perished far away, and the women are careless and do not tend him. Servants will no longer work honestly of their own accord, when their masters are not there to give them orders; for Zeus the far-thunderer takes away half a man's virtue, when the day of slavery descends upon him.' So saying, he entered the lordly house, and went straight to the hall and in among the haughty wooers. As for Argus, the doom of black death came upon him then and there, when he had seen Odysseus again after nineteen years.

First to see the swineherd as he made his way through the hall was godlike Telemachus, and at once he signed with his head to summon him. The swineherd looked around and found a stool lying handy, on which the carver used to sit cutting portions of meat in plenty for the wooers when they feasted in the hall. This he took and carried to Telemachus' table, and placed it opposite to him, and sat down himself.

THE POETIC MEDIUM

In introducing the preceding passages the purpose has been to illustrate by example how both in *Iliad* and in *Odyssey* the facts of the story are made to speak for themselves by stimulating the hearer's faculty of recognition: they have in themselves the power to interest or excite or move, and can do so still when communicated in plain prose. The poetical dress of metre and language and style and manner and artifice in which, in the original, the exposition of the facts is clothed is really a separable element. It provides throughout an agreeable and interesting accompaniment, as it were, to the telling of the story and at appropriate moments and in varying degrees enhances its vividness or its emotive value. The ways and means of this are subject of what follows.

(i) Verse-form

The rhythmical unit of Homeric poetry is a line of six metrical feet (hexameter), of which the last consists always of two syllables in the form − ⌣̄ (a long syllable followed by one that may be either short or long), while all or any of the first five may consist either of three syllables in the form − ⌣ ⌣ (dactyl: a long syllable followed by two short) or of two syllables in the form − − (spondee: two longs). The value of a syllable as long or short is determined strictly by the nature of the vowel and the consonant or consonants following it: a naturally short vowel followed by two consecutive consonants acquires in most circumstances the metrical value of a naturally long one. This value is unaffected by the stress, light or heavy, that may be given it in pronunciation: 'unity' or 'density' in this system would be true dactyls, but 'misery' or 'meaningful' or 'mesmerize' would not. It results that the metrical pattern of the verse has a strictness and precision that a system based on stress in pronunciation cannot match.

The length of the hexameter line is enough to enable a succession of such lines to flow, rather than stepping, but also short enough to keep the metrical pattern well defined. Moreover, the availability of dactyl and spondee as alternatives in each of the first five feet makes possible a great variety of speed and movement. The line may contain anything from twelve to seventeen syllables (compared with the fairly stable ten or eleven of the most familiar narrative metre in English), and any of thirty-two different possible arrangements of dactyl and spondee in combination: already in the first eleven lines of the *Iliad* ten different such combinations occur. Dactyls (− ⌣ ⌣) usually predominate in these constantly changing arrangements, and the result combines variety with a notable ease and speed of flow. This ease and speed of flow is assisted by the fact that the Homeric language abounds in vowels separated by single consonants or following immediately on

one another; collocations of double and triple consonants being pro-
portionally fewer, though readily enough available for special effects.
The difference between Homer's language and ours in this respect
can be seen when it is considered that the first fourteen lines of the
Iliad in a well-known English verse translation contain about three
times as many collocations of two or three or more consecutive consonants as they do in the original: or if the first line of *Paradise Lost*,
'Of man's first disobedience and the fruit . . .' is compared with the
first line of the *Iliad* (*mēnin aeide, theā, Pēlēiadĕ̄o Achilēos*), in which
no vowel is separated from another by more than a single consonant.[48]

(ii) Poetic diction

The language of the Homeric poems, though of course it must have
been familiar and easily intelligible, in essentials, to the ordinary
people who were to listen to it, was not a language that was spoken
in ordinary life. This is clear from the fact that it uses indifferently,
as metrically convenient alternatives, forms of common words that
belonged properly to different dialects or different stages of a dialect's
development: alternative forms, for instance, of the words for 'you'
and 'we', for the verb 'to be', for the numerals 'one' (in the feminine)
and 'four', for the genitive case of Achilles' surname when he is called
'son of Peleus', for the dative case of the words for 'hands' and 'feet';
and so on. Many other examples could be cited, but those given should
suffice to show that the language of the poems is a mixture of elements
that would not normally be found in employment side by side. It is
a mixture that cannot have been a sudden creation, but must have
been developed (by a process which we can no longer trace) in the
practice of a succession of poets over a considerable period of time.
As such, it will have been fully familiar to our poet and his hearers,
but at the same time unmistakably separate and different from the
language of everyday communication. But the separation was one that
had arisen naturally, and not by a deliberate effort to achieve an
elevation of tone uncontaminated by prosaic associations. Consequently the Homeric language can accept familiar words and manners
of speech from the life of everyday, as well as the elaborately honorific
terms of heroic tradition.[49] It can catch the tone of exchanges between
beggars as well as between noblemen, and the conversational styles of
children and servants no less than those of lords and ladies and warriors. In the *Odyssey* the young princess Nausicaa says (in Homeric

language but a quite evidently familiar tone) to her father (*Odyssey* 6.57): 'Dear Papa, please have the waggon harnessed for me; there are fine clothes of ours lying all dirty and I want to take them down to the river to wash them.' In Pope's version (actually the lines are those of his collaborator Broome) this passage runs:

> Will my dread sire his ear attentive deign,
> And may his child the royal car obtain?
> Say, with thy garments shall I wend my way
> Where through the vales the mazy waters stray?

A modern will not feel the need that Pope's generation felt to elevate the tone. But he will also not find it easy to preserve an element of poetry in his rendering.[50]

(iii) Word-length and word-sound*

The Homeric vocabulary is very copious.[51] As well as alternative forms of many words (such as *dōma* and *dō* for 'house', *krithai* and *krī* for 'barley', *dexiteros* and *dexios* for 'on the right hand', *cheiressi* and *chersi*, *podessi* and *possi*, etc.), and alternative terms for many things (three words for 'sword' (*xiphos*, *āor*, *phasganon*) and four for 'helmet' (*korus*, *kuneē*, *truphaleia*, *pēlēx*) and five for 'spear' (*doru*, *xuston*, *meliē*, *enchos*, *aichmē*), etc.), it includes some fifty words for different parts of the body, and some fifty-five that signify varieties of sound (such as *klangē*, *ēchē*, *kanachē*, *bromos*, *doupos*, *alalētos*, *ololūgē*, *orumagdos*, *oimōgē*, *kōkutos*, *bebrūchōs*, *keklēgōs*, *kanchaloōn*, etc.). It has at its disposal a stock of monosyllabic particles (such as *toi*, *pou*, *per*, *nun*, *de*, *men*, *an*, *ke*, *de*, *te*, *ge*, *ar*, *ra*), of which some can be inserted or omitted at will with slight effect upon the sense, and some can lose their final vowel by elision and so be reduced to the value of a single consonant. It has also at its disposal an abundance of words of four syllables and more, in contrast with the predominance in English of monosyllables and disyllables: thus in the first fourteen lines of *Iliad* 18 a good modern English translation uses 160 words against 100 in the Greek; and while the English has only two words of four syllables, and none longer, the Greek has ten words of four syllables and eight of five. In consequence the Greek has great possibilities of variety of texture and of managed emphasis. And this wide range of word-length in the Homeric vocabulary is matched by

*for a conventional pronunciation see p. 99.

a correspondingly wide range of word-sound. On the one hand there is frequent juxtaposition of vowels without intervening consonants (*ēelioio, aoidiaousa, pithoi oinoio palaiou hēdupotoio*); on the other hand there is plentiful provision for hard consonants in staccato sequences (*patagos de te gignet' odontōn*) and harsh combinations (*ex auchen' eaxe, adzēchēs orumagdos, trichtha te kai tetrachtha, lax en stēthesi bās exespase meilinon enchos*). Many possibilities of assonance are available, and evidently favoured by the poet's ear: thus, there is frequent duplication both of vowels and consonants (*tode moi krēēnon eëldor; lelachēte, alalēmai,* etc.); there is rhyme from similar inflexions juxtaposed (*hēphi biēphi, krueroio gooio*) or separated (*Iliad* 5.161 and 239) *hōs de leōn en bousi thorōn; hōs ara phonēsantes, es harmata poikila bantes*); there are repetitions of consonantal sounds in their harder and softer varieties (*ton d'apameibomenos*); there is insistent alliteration on single initial consonants (*Iliad* 18.452) (*pempe de min polemonde, polun d'hama lāon opasse*); there are, occasionally, very elaborate repetitions of whole groups of vowels and consonants together ((*Odyssey* 3.272) *tēn d'ethelōn ethelousan anēgagen honde domonde*; (*Iliad* 18.553) *alla d'amallodetēres en elledanoisi deonto*); and many other varieties.

(iv) Simplicity and lucidity

The style of the poems is plain and lucid, both in its sentence-structure and in the way in which individual words are used. Its naturalness in these respects can be judged from the ease with which it can be translated at sight into English by anyone who has acquired a fair command of Homeric grammar and vocabulary. As a general rule, sentences are kept short. Subordinate clauses are comparatively few, and follow more often than they precede the sentence to which they are attached. Within the sentence the order of words is readily varied, with the freedom that an inflected language permits; but words that naturally belong together, such as noun and epithet, are never far separated from one another, and usually stand in juxtaposition. Adjectives are used in their normal applications: even mild departures from the norm (such as 'pale fear' or 'pitiless bronze') are few and far between. Metaphors too ('black cloud of grief', 'tamed by the scourge of Zeus', etc.) are relatively infrequent, and, though sometimes forcible, are always brief and easy to absorb: there is no subtle or elaborate imagery of the kind that requires peculiar sensibility or an effort of the intellect for its apprehension. Similes are either short and simple or extended and explicit, so that in either case their effect is easily taken in.

Homeric poetry is thus eminently easy to understand. It is also eminently easy to follow, because the order of thought or happening is clear and consequent and sign-posted throughout by the use of logical connectives and by demonstratives or other guide-words positioned early in each sentence. The resulting clarity is one cause why Homeric narrative is felt to move so swiftly; for what seems swift to reader or hearer is what neither outruns nor is outrun by his understanding— brevity of expression, as such, does not necessarily assist speed of comprehension, but may indeed be inimical to it. The Homeric style is economical of words in that it frequently omits a term which serves a purely syntactical purpose and which the imagination instantly supplies when the syntax is left incomplete. On the other hand it may appear lavish of words, in that it admits a fair number of archaic tautologies ('when they were assembled and gathered together', 'they gave heed and obeyed', 'in his heart and in his mind', etc.) and otio- sities ('saw with his eyes', 'heard with his ears', etc.), and a large number of conventional epithets, and some occasionally conspicuous repetitions of what has been said before. These habits however do not seem to retard the pace of the narrative or generate impatience, but rather, by loosening a little the texture of the style and varying its tempo, to make it easier to take in. They have moreover a certain positive value, both in their own right, and as constituents of a dis- tinctive 'manner' appropriate to the kind of poetry that epic is. Of two of the constituents of this manner more now needs to be said.

(v) Conventional epithets

By a 'conventional' epithet is meant here an epithet which is introduced without any necessary relevance to its context. It usually refers to a permanent or typical attribute of the thing or person mentioned. When at the beginning of the *Iliad* it is said that the *baneful* wrath of Achilles brought many *stalwart* heroes to their death, the epithets in their context have a function of significance to perform; and it is a proper piece of description when we are told that Chryses came car- rying a *golden* staff, and so on. But when the poet says that Chryses came to the *swift* ships of the Achaeans, and that Agamemnon bade him begone from the *hollow* ships and not return, and later that the *white-armed* goddess Hera inspired the summoning of an assembly, at which *swift-footed* Achilles stood up to speak—in these instances the epithets serve no specific purpose where they stand, but are simply products of a stylistic habit. This habit, with many of the combinations of noun and epithet resulting from it, was certainly ancient and traditional when the *Iliad* and *Odyssey* came into being, a part of an inherited stock-in-trade of the makers of epic poetry. The habit owed both its origin, in part, and its persistence to the help it afforded in the process of impromptu composition; for the epithet may be put in or left out at will, and various epithets attached to and in agreement with the various grammatical cases of the same noun can furnish a welcome abundance of resources to meet the requirements of metre and grammar in different contexts.[52] For example, there occur in the *Iliad* and *Odyssey* together nearly seventy different combinations of epithets (swift, black, curved, even-trimmed, hollow, dark-prowed, long-oared, sea-faring, etc., etc.) with the word for 'ship' (or 'ships') in its various cases, singular and plural; and almost every one of these combinations has a metrical value different from that of any other. But such abundant provision is exceptional; and while some proper names, especially, are provided with a wide range of epithets of this kind, in many instances only one combination of noun and epithet occurs, and that not always with frequency.

It may be asked: what effect or value do these epithets have, beyond lending a distinctive manner to the Homeric style? The typical property of the thing or person mentioned that they refer to is commonly something that evokes a response of recognition or interest or admiration or pleasure or dismay. Consequently they convey collectively a positive though diffused awareness of the world in which the stories unfold, which is in some aspects a world lit with the splendour of a heroic past, but in others the same world that we still know ourselves, though our sensitivity to its beauty and interest may have been dulled by the influence of contemporary culture. Thus while Homeric narrative focuses (as we have seen) on the particular in the selection of facts that it reports, the conventional epithets lend it a colour and brilliance that is general and pervasive. And so, without insistence, we are called to awareness

of the wide expanse of sky, bright sun, shining moon; black earth, bearing grain, giving life; landscapes with shadow-traversed hills, eddying rivers, hollow caves, windswept headlands, deep harbours; the boundless sea, heaving and murmuring, misty, grey or violet-blue;

of windswept Troy, fertile Phthia, sandy Pylos, rocky Ithaca, Mycenae rich in gold;

of white milk, white barley-meal, pale-yellow honey, smooth-flowing oil of olive, red wine that warms the heart;

of white-tusked boars, tawny lions, antlered deer; oxen straight-horned or crook-horned, broad-browed, shambling; bleating goats and fat, white-fleeced sheep; dogs with noisy bark and sharp, tearing teeth; horses with heads held proudly high, and flowing manes and clattering hooves, neighing, snorting, galloping;

of towns set on steep hills, with strong walls and high gates, and spacious streets and squares within; great halls with high-raftered roofs, full of sounds and shadows, with thresholds of trimmed stone and brightly decorated doors opening on courtyards with echoing colonnades; chairs and tables and store-chests of finished workmanship;

of ships that sail the sea, fast-faring, with hollow hulls and many benches and long banks of oars and beaked, red-painted prows; brazen mail-coats, bright breast plates, shining helmets, horsehair plumes, bossed shields of bronze or oxhide; long spears, bronze-pointed, massive, deadly, flying straight to their mark, casting long shadows; bent bows and feathered arrows, sharp swords with silver-studded hilts; bronze, bright and sharp and cruel;

of men who are strong, great-hearted, noble; proud squires and trusty followers; women with braided hair, bright eyes, soft cheeks, white arms, trim-girdled waists, neat ankles, flowing gowns;

of glorious Achilles fleet of foot, great Hector of the glittering helmet, huge Ajax son of Telamon, Zeus gatherer of the clouds and lord of lightning, golden Aphrodite, white-armed Hera, Poseidon shaker of the earth, saffron-robed Dawn, silver-footed Thetis; and many other gods and heroes with attributes of grandeur or romance or noble lineage.

(vi) Recurrent lines and phrases

The second hall-mark of the Homeric manner, not less conspicuous than the dispensable epithet, is the habit of repetition: the repetition, occasional or frequent or very frequent, of the same phrase (or line, or set of lines) in a variety of contexts. Many of the phrases thus repeatedly occurring are combinations of noun and dispensable epithet; so that these two characteristics of style, the dispensable epithet and the recurrent phrase, to some extent can be seen to coincide. But the coincidence is only partial. On the one hand there are plenty of dispensable epithets in the *Iliad* and *Odyssey* which in these poems at least do not recur. On the other hand the habit of repetition is by no means confined to noun-epithet combinations, but embraces a great variety of other kinds of phrase—such as (to take a single obvious instance) the many stock lines or phrases that are used to introduce a speaker's words or his hearer's reaction to them. It also embraces many word-groups, too numerous and various to be exemplified here, that are adaptable to a number of different positions in the hexameter line. And there are other groups, extending beyond the limits of a single line, which can be adapted to various contexts by variation of key words within them, as for example (*Iliad* 6.492; *Odyssey* 1.358, 21.352), 'But war (*or* the word of authority *or* the bow) shall be for men to manage, and for me not least, of all that are in Ilium (*or* for I am master in this house).'

The extent to which this habit of repetition operates can be illustrated by reference to the known number of repetitions of complete lines, which are of course substantially fewer than the repetitions of shorter phrases. The *Iliad* and *Odyssey* together comprise approximately 28,000 lines; the *Iliad* about 16,000, the *Odyssey* about 12,000. Of these roughly 2,000 different lines recur once or more, and with their recurrences make some 5,500 lines, or about one-fifth of the whole. Looked at from one point of view, this means that every fifth line of the poems on average has occurred or will occur again. But looked at from another point of view it means that the average recurrence of any one of the basic 2,000 different recurring lines is less than twice in a total of 28,000, a frequency hardly enough to excite attention. But the frequency of recurrence is very far from even. A limited number of recurring lines recur often or very often indeed: the great majority recur once or twice only. The modern reader is hardly aware of this last and largest category; nor aware of anything odd or awkward about passages such as *Odyssey* 5. 1–50 or *Iliad* 8. 39–70 which on nearer view are found to consist as to two-thirds of lines which appear also in other places in *Iliad* or *Odyssey*. On the other hand certain repetitions, extensive or very frequent, are at once felt as obvious, and so become a constituent of the distinctive epic manner.

These are of several kinds. First, there is repetition at length by a speaker of another speaker's (or his own or the narrator's) earlier words, as when (to cite two instances out of more than a dozen)

Agamemnon in *Iliad* 2 repeats verbatim to the assembled chiefs the injunction (in sixteen lines) that he has just received from the deceptive Dream, or Telemachus in *Odyssey* 4 repeats verbatim to Menelaus the request (in ten lines) that he has addressed to Nestor in the previous book.

Secondly, there is the very frequent repetition of some noun-epithet combinations, notably ones relating to ships ('black ship' occurs at line-endings some thirty times), and to bronze ('with the sharp bronze' more than thirty times), and to the names of characters who figure prominently in the stories: 'Zeus cloud-gatherer', 'fleet-foot Achilles', 'resourceful Odysseus', 'Hector of the glittering helmet', and so on.

Thirdly, there are the familiar phrases with which speech is introduced or concluded: 'And to him . . . speaking uttered winged words' (more than fifty times), 'And . . . answered him and said . . .', 'And . . . looked angrily at him and said . . .', 'So he spoke and . . . was not unheedful', and many others.

Fourthly, there are single lines and short groups of lines which describe events that are recurrent, either generally in all life or in the particular setting of the story being told: reflection, decision, the exchange of meaning looks; sunrise and sunset; travelling by land or sea; beginning and ending a meal; reception of a guest at table; the fall of men in battle and their movements in action—alighting from a chariot, striding forward through the fray, aiming and casting a spear, avoiding an enemy's stroke.

These conspicuous recurrences contribute, as has already been said, to give the epic style its characteristic formal manner. But they have also as a rule—at least those of the second and third and fourth varieties—a value of their own, which no doubt accounts for their selection and survival in a role that gives them extra prominence. This most commonly is a simple quality of euphony (as for instance in *ton d'apameibomenos*), but sometimes also of picturesqueness ('winged words', 'rose-fingered Dawn'), or typical expressiveness ('the sun set and all the ways were darkened'; 'they went on board and took their places and sitting in order beat the grey sea with their oars'). But perhaps there is more to be said. In a long sea journey days pass and sleep and waking succeed one another with a uniformity that becomes monotonous because unrelieved. In physical conflict the decisive cut or thrust or blow will occur as an incident among many actions that are repeated again and again in changing combinations. Every life, however interesting and varied includes the regularly re-

curring cycle of bedtime and mealtimes and time of rising, together
with an abundance of thoughts and actions and modes of speech that
occur less regularly but not less often. The typical and the individual,
the generic and the unique, are the warp and weft of all human experience. From this point of view the admixture of repetitive elements
in the Homeric style can be felt to correspond to the texture of life
itself, and that timelessly—though one of the repetitive elements, the
honorific epithets attached to the names of so many of the participants, relates it specifically to the life of the heroic age.[53]

(vii) Resources of poetic emphasis

The preceding sections of this essay have been concerned with certain
general properties of the poetic dress in which Homeric narrative is
clad. The verse-form and the sounds in the language provide that
narrative, as has been observed, with a continuously agreeable ac-
companiment. A specialized but uncontrived poetic vocabulary
separates it from the commonplace without rejecting the familiar.
Clarity and simplicity of expression make it easy to absorb, and co-
operate with the flow of the metre to give it a rapid movement. Some
conspicuous elements in the style give it a distinctive manner, and
enliven its fabric with general qualities of colour and texture. There
remains the question of poetic emphasis, of the means by which particular effects are obtained at particular moments, to add vividness
to description or intensity to the expression of feeling. These prove
to be few, and sparingly employed.

(a) Rhythm and sound assisting sense *

Chief of these resources is the adaptation of rhythm and word-sound
to the positive reinforcement of meaning (as opposed to the provision
of a pleasant but unrelated accompaniment). Thus, description may be
assisted by special movements of the verse, resulting sometimes from
different relations of pauses in the syntax of statement to pauses in
the metrical pattern, and sometimes from different divisions of metrical
feet between words. Examples will be found in the accounts of
Pandarus' bow-shot (*Iliad* 4. 116–26), and the shattering of Odysseus'
raft (*Odyssey* 5. 365–76), and Odysseus' embarcation on the Phaeacian
ship that brings him home (*Odyssey* 13. 73–80), and his dramatic feat
of archery that precedes the slaying of the suitors (*Odyssey* 21. 412–
24); or again in a comparison between the lines that describe respect-

*for a conventional pronunciation see p. 99

ively the bounding downhill course of Sisyphus' stone (*autis epeita pedonde kulindeto lāas anaidēs: Odyssey* 11. 598) and the death of the dog Argus (*Argon d'au kata moir' elaben melanos thanatoio: Odyssey* 17. 326).

Another aid to expression may come from the weight or lightness of the syllables in a verse, or from their smoothness or harshness, or the combined effect of both kinds of quality. The heavy movement of *psūchēn kiklēskōn Patroklēos deiloio* (*Iliad* 23. 221), with its maximum possible of long syllables and abundance of juxtaposed consonants, is appropriate to the long-drawn cries with which the mourning Achilles calls on his dead friend's ghost.[54] The almost equally heavy movement of *err' ek nēsou thāsson, elenchiste dzōontōn* (*Odyssey* 10. 72), with its similarly weighted syllables and the growling and booming quality of some of them, is appropriate to the stern and menacing tone of Aeolus' dismissal of the unfortunate Odysseus. The harsh sounds in the line *lax en stēthesi bās exespase meilinon enchos* (*Iliad* 6. 65) accords with the harshness of the act, as the warrior plants his heel on his victim's chest and wrenches out the spear from the death-wound. On the other hand the dactylic and unimpeded movement of *alla ti moi tōn ēdos, epei philos ōleth' hetairos?* (*Iliad* 18. 80) lends itself to pronunciation as an elegiac wail, as Achilles' grief rushes to find expression to his mother after he learns of Patroclus' death. And in *rimph' epheron thoon harma . . .* (*Iliad* 17. 458) the run of dactyls and the lightly aspirated consonants and absence of naturally long vowels help to convey the tripping run of the chariot that is being described. Again in *histia de sphin trichtha te kai tetrachtha dieschisen īs anemoio* (*Odyssey* 9. 70–1) the quality of the consonant and vowel sounds comes near to a positive suggestion of what is happening, as the piercing blast of the squall rips the sails to tatters. Positively expressive also is the onomatopoeic quality of many individual words: for instance the equivalents of 'clattered' (*arabēse*), 'thudded' (*doupēse*), 'wailed' (*kōkūse*), 'whimpering' (*knuzēthmos*), 'bleating' (*blēchē*), etcetera—but Homeric stock is larger than the English and its words more striking.

Again, many Homeric words give impact to their meaning by exhibiting exceptional length or unusual sound-values: thus the ideas expressed in English by 'scheme', 'capsize', 'rising to a crest', 'beat back' are rendered in the Homeric vocabulary by strong-wounding words of five or six or even seven syllables apiece (*bussodomeuō, anakumbaliadzō, phalērioōnta, apostuphelidzō*); and the piercing cry of Achilles when he hears of Patroclus' death (*Iliad* 18. 35) is rendered by two strong words of four and three syllables in succession (*smerdaleon d'ōmōxe*). A long and striking word in an emphatic position may serve to give a strong effect at a point of special significance—the awful consequences of Achilles' wrath (*oulomenēn: Iliad* 1. 2), the brilliance of the supernatural flame that lights Achilles' head when he makes his dramatic appearance at the moat of the camp (*pamphanoōsan: Iliad* 18. 206), the murderous hands of Achilles that Priam brings himself to kiss (*deinous, androphonous: Iliad* 24. 479), the miserable condition of humanity that Zeus pities as he looks down on the battlefield (*ou men gar ti pou estin oïdzurōteron andros . . .: Iliad* 17. 446).

In the instances so far considered there are, superficially at least, identifiable reasons why the sound and rhythm of the language may be felt to assist the expression of what is to be conveyed. But it is not always so. There are many passages in which co-operation of sound and sense is extremely powerful in its effect, but no rationally explicable relationship between the two can be detected: one can only say that a remarkably emotive situation as the poet perceives it has generated remarkable qualities of sound and rhythm in the combinations of words that come to his mind. As for instance in the description of the Trojan camp-fires at the end of *Iliad* 8. (562–5):

> A thousand fires were burning on the plain, and by each
> sat fifty men in the glare of the blazing flames;
> and the horses champing white barley and millet
> stood by the chariots, waiting for bright-throned Dawn.

The Greek here runs:

> *chīli ar' en pediō pura kaieto, par de hekastō*
> *hēato pentēkonta selā puros aithomenoio.*
> *hippoi de krī leukon ereptomenoi kai olūras*
> *hestaotes par ochesphin eüthronon Ēō mimnon.*

Or again, the last words of dying Hector to Achilles in *Iliad* 22 (358–360):

> Take heed now lest I bring god's wrath upon you
> on the day when Paris and Phoebus Apollo
> shall slay you, strong though you are, at the Scaean gate.

The Greek runs:

> *phrazeo nun, mē toi ti theōn mēnima genōmai*
> *ēmati tō hote ken se Paris kai Phoibos Apollōn*
> *esthlon eont' olesōsin eni Skaiēsi pulēsi.*

It is easy to feel the effect, and (on inspection) to observe the fact of the strong but unobtrusive assonances in both these passages, and of the unusual metrical pattern in the last two lines of the former of them. But it is hard to discover in either case an intellectually explicable relationship between this effect and the effect of the content of the statement, which undoubtedly it enhances.

The case is similar with joyful Eurycleia's summons to Penelope in *Odyssey* 23. 52–7:

> But come with me, that you may enter on your happiness,
> with full hearts, both of you. For you have suffered
>   much.
> And now what you craved so long has come to pass.
> He lives, and is here, returned, at his own hearth;
>   and he has found you
> and your son too, safe at home; and on those who
>   wronged him
> and wooed his wife—in this his house he has taken
>   vengeance on them all.

The Greek runs:

> *all' hepeu, ophra sphōin eüphrosunēs epibēton*
> *amphoterō philon ētor, epei kaka polla pepasthe.*
> *nun d'ēdē tode makron eëldor ektetelestai.*
> *ēlthe men autos dzōos ephestios, heure de kai se*
> *kai paid'en megaroisi, kakōs d'hoi per min eredzon*
> *mnēstēres, tous pantas etisato hō eni oikō.*

Here three lines full of unusual assonances are followed by three that are charged with rhetorically affective rhythm.

(b) 'Figures' of word-arrangement

Most of the 'figures' of word-arrangement that later rhetoric has made familiar appear already in the Homeric poems, some common, and some rare. They serve to lend variety or interest or energy to the diction, and also, when appropriate, to enhance emotion. A simple type is the omission of connectives in a series: 'Swords fine to see, black-bound, well-hilted', or 'A spear ponderous, huge, massive'. The opposite of this is an accumulation of connectives: 'Do you not see the man that I too am, how tall and how handsome, and I am son of a noble father, and a goddess is the mother who bore me? A time will come—or dawn, or eve, or noon—when . . .' (*Iliad* 21. 108 ff.). Another simple figure is repetition of the same word at the beginning of successive clauses, or sentences: 'Thrice he . . . and thrice he . . .', or 'So he spoke; and many of them that heard were willing to go with him. Willing were the two Ajaxes, squires of the war-god, willing was Meriones, and right willing was Nestor's son, and willing was Atreus' son, spear-famed Menelaus, and willing too was Odysseus, that man much-enduring . . .' (*Iliad* 10.227 ff.). Then again there may be repetition of the same word differently compounded or differently declined: 'Unhappy father of a hapless child', or 'They made a fence of spear with spear, shield with shield firm-planted, buckler to buckler, helmet to helmet, man to man' (*Iliad* 13.130). A figure rarely used is the echoing of a phrase in successive clauses: 'With him is no soft speaking as of man with maid, as man and maid speak soft with one another' (*Iliad* 22.127). Another, also rare, is arrangement in the order ABBA: 'The bowstring to his breast he drew and to the bow-stave the iron arrow-head' (*Iliad* 4.123). Then, too, there is apostrophizing of a person in the story: 'Him then you mocked, Patroclus, saying . . .' (*Iliad* 16.744). There is the rhetorical question which expects no answer or is answered by the questioner himself: 'Which of the gods then was it that roused those two to quarrel? The son of Leto and of Zeus it was'. And there is the patterning of an elaborate sentence with phrases and clauses set in parallel: 'My friend, if you and I, this war survived, could live for ever, ageless and immortal, then would I neither fight myself among the foremost, nor yet bid you seek honour in the battle; but now, since death is always near at hand, from perils numberless which no man born can escape or evade, come let us give some man his chance of glory, or let some man give ours to us' (*Iliad* 12.322 ff.).

Severally or in combination these arrangements appear often, as above, in pathetic or otherwise emotive contexts. Thus, in Hector's thoughts for his wife: 'But not so much for the Trojans is my concern, nor even for Hecuba, nor for King Priam, nor for my brothers . . . as for you . . .' (*Iliad* 6.450 ff.). And in Nestor's thoughts of the friends who fell at Troy: 'There lies the warrior Ajax, and there Achilles, and there Patroclus, peer of gods in counsel, and there my own son, strong and handsome, Antilochus, fastest runner and bravest fighter' (*Odyssey* 3.109 ff.). Or in the pursuit of Hector by Achilles before their final combat: 'That way they ran, the two, one fleeing, one pursuing; in front a strong man fled, but pursuing him ran one far stronger' (*Iliad* 22.157 ff.). These resources of style are used with economy, but they are all already at command.

(c) Metaphors

Metaphors are always very simple, and scarce too, with the exception of a few that are embedded in recurrent phrases. These last have an archaic and picturesque quality which make them an ingredient of the distinctive Homeric manner. Such are 'winged words', 'the barrier of the teeth', 'shepherd of the people', 'marrow of men' (barley-meal), 'mother of flocks' (a land of rich pastures), 'threshold of old age', 'fatness of ploughland', 'dalliance of foremost fighters', 'don a coat of stones' (be stoned to death), weapons 'eager to gorge on flesh of men'. One or two evidently ancient and traditional metaphors are of uncertain meaning: 'dykes of war', 'drawing taut over both the rope of ruin'. Other metaphors are less exotic in character. An angry man's heart 'seethes with gall', and men say of him 'surely your mother suckled you with gall'. A speaker 'begins to weave his counsel'. Men in vexation 'eat their hearts'. An arrow 'leaps' from the bowstring. A battlefield 'shivers with brazen spears'. A berserk warrior's spear 'rages'. Dancers' feet 'twinkle'. The earth, as soldiers march out to war, 'laughs with the glitter of bronze'. The sky 'blares aloud' (like a trumpet) with the echo of a hero's shout. The king of the gods is 'dispenser of war's chances'. A brave ally is 'the city's prop and stay'. A good fighter is 'a bulwark in the battle'. Defenders 'fence their ships with a barrier of bronze'. A beaten army is 'tamed and broken by the scourge of Zeus'. A man who wastes his talent is 'an idle burden on the earth'. Some men 'take the gift of sleep', some 'sleep the sleep of bronze', on some descends 'a black cloud of grief', on some 'the black cloud that is death'. A man unmoved by pity (but also a man unmoved by fear) 'has in his breast a heart of iron'.

In a single case a metaphor begins to be elaborated, when Odysseus (*Iliad* 19. 221 ff.) says that 'in war the bronze strews straw in plenty on the ground; but the harvest of grain is little indeed when the scales are turned'.

(d) Similes

The similes in Homer are of two kinds, one brief and simple like the Homeric metaphors, the other (the typical Homeric simile) extended so as to become in itself a little picture or story.

The first kind, like metaphor, is sparingly employed. The god Ares' war-cry is 'like the howl of a sudden squall'. An assault of warriors is 'like a dark tempest's blast'. A smitten man falls from a battlement head first 'like a diver'. The words of an eloquent speaker come thick and fast 'like snow flakes in a blizzard'. The activity of spinning and weaving women in a workroom is like the (shimmering of the) 'leaves of a tall poplar'. The sound of the voices of old men talking together is 'like the chirring of crickets'. The speed of the magic ships of the Phaeacians is 'swift as thought or flying arrow'. The texture of a finely woven garment is 'glossy as an onion-skin'. A plucked bow-string sounds 'like the note of a swallow' in a silent hall. Odysseus' expression when, unable to reveal himself, he controls his emotion in the presence of his weeping wife is 'set as firm as horn or iron'. Agamemnon's eyes 'flash like fire' in his anger at the seer's revelation in the assembly scene at the beginning of the Iliad. Achilles' eyes 'glare like fire' in his lust for battle when he sees the god-made armour brought him by his mother. As he arms himself later his shield 'shines like the moon' and his helmet 'glitters like a star', and his armour when he tries himself in it 'seems to lift him like wings'. And so Hector and Hector's father and mother see him, 'gleaming in bronze bright as blazing fire or rising sun', as he draws near across the plain and Hector waits for him beneath the wall of Troy. Two more distinctive comparisons are put in the mouth of Achilles himself. He has, he says, served and enriched Agamemnon for poor reward 'like a bird that brings morsels to its unfledged chicks, and itself goes hungry'. And he realizes too late the insidious pleasure that there is in indulging anger 'sweeter than honey', and the suddenness with which anger grows and swells 'like smoke'.

The extended simile, but for its uneven distribution in the poems, might well have been included earlier among the distinctive ingredients of the Homeric 'manner'. It is much more frequent in the *Iliad* (about 200 examples in about 16,000 lines) than in the *Odyssey* (about 40 in 12,000 lines). This difference of frequency corresponds to the difference of subject between the two poems; for it (the difference of frequency) occurs also within the same poem between different parts. Nearly one-third of the total of extended similes in the *Odyssey* are comprised in two episodes, the shipwreck and escape of Odysseus in the fifth book and his self-disclosure and slaying of the suitors in the twenty-first and twenty-second. In the *Iliad* the first book has no extended simile at all, and the sixth, ninth, and twenty-fourth have only two apiece: all these have their setting in camp or city. On the other hand, the battle-scenes of the sixteenth and seventeenth books— the story of Patroclus' feats of war and death and the fighting over his body—contain some forty extended similes, of which five are concentrated at the end, in the last thirty-five lines.

The typical uses of the extended simile are three: to suggest inward feelings and states of mind, obviously not capable of direct description; to express, by visible illustration, distinctive qualities attaching to individual things or actions or processes; and to render effects of multitude and mass.

The first of these is equally a requirement in both the poems: the relief of the Trojans when Hector reappears on the battlefield is like that of tired sailors welcoming a breeze when they are exhausted with long rowing (*Iliad* 7. 4 ff.); the astonishment of those present when Priam appears in Achilles' hut is like that excited by the sudden arrival of a fugitive seeking protection in some great man's house (*Iliad* 24. 480 ff.); the impatience of Odysseus waiting for sundown in Alcinous' palace is like that of a ploughman eager for his supper towards the end of a long day's work (*Odyssey* 13. 31 ff.); the wavering of Penelope's troubled thoughts, undecided whether to abandon at last her resistance to proposals of remarriage, is like the wavering note of a plaintively singing bird (*Odyssey* 19. 518 ff.).

The other two typical uses of the extended simile—to render distinctive qualities in actions (especially) and effects of mass—have an obvious special relevance to the long battle scenes of the *Iliad*. Hector, recovered from the effects of a blow which laid him unconscious, returns refreshed to the fighting like a well-fed stallion that has broken its tether and goes galloping exultant, with head high and mane tossing (*Iliad* 15. 263 ff.); Antilochus leaps forward to strip the armour from a fallen man like a hunter's dog leaping on a beast that the hunter has brought down (*Iliad* 15. 579 ff.); the god Apollo tumbles the wall of the camp as easily and nonchalantly as a child playing by the sea side tumbles a sand castle (*Iliad* 15. 362 ff.); the battle-front is as straight and steady as a carpenter's rule when he is cutting a long timber for a ship (*Iliad* 15. 410 ff.); the impact of Hector's charge on the embattled Greeks is like that of a wave breaking over a ship in a storm, deluging it with spray, while the wind roars in the sail and the sailors fear for their lives (*Iliad* 15. 624 ff.); and when Hector kills one man the others scatter like cattle when a lion springs on a beast in the middle of a moving herd while the herdsman is guarding front or rear (*Iliad* 15. 630 ff.). When the Greek army moves out of its encampment to form for battle on the plain (*Iliad* 2. 455–483), a succession of five similes makes the process visible in as many several aspects. In the same way five similes help to describe the scene when Menelaus and Meriones carry the body of Patroclus off the field, their retreat covered by the Ajaxes against the fury of the advancing Trojans (*Iliad* 17. 725–59). In the Odyssey the timbers of Odysseus' raft are scattered all ways by a great wave as a chaff-heap is scattered by a puff of wind (*Odyssey* 5. 368). Odysseus strings his great bow as easily as a musician fits a new string to a lyre (*Odyssey* 21. 406). He stands all bloodied among the slain suitors like a lion that has just fed on its kill (*Odyssey* 22. 402).

The details in an extended simile are not always directly relevant to the point of the comparison being made, though they serve to complete or reinforce the picture which contains it. For example, Achilles confronted by Aeneas as he enters the battle is described (*Iliad* 20. 164–73) as follows:

> And from the other side Peleus' son leapt forward to meet him, like a marauding lion whom men have set out to kill, all the men of a village banded together; and he at first comes on regardless, but when one of the young braves hits him with a spear-cast, suddenly he crouches and shows his fangs, foaming, and his heart within him growls for fury, and he lashes his flanks and hind-quarters with his tail to left and right, as he rouses himself to do battle, and, eyes aglare, goes charging forward to slay his man or be slain himself in the foremost of the fray.

Evidently enough there is much in these particulars that does not correspond to anything in the situation or the conduct of Achilles; though they all contribute cumulatively to make real the picture of the angry lion, which is to make real by illustration the anger of Achilles and its menace.

Many of the similes however have a multiple relevance, several of the particulars in the simile corresponding to several elements in the situation it illustrates. In the *Iliad*, when battle is joined again after the abortive duel between Paris and Menelaus and the breaking of the truce, the advance of the Greek army (*Iliad* 4. 422 ff.) is compared to a succession of waves at sea, rolling onward one behind another and then breaking on the shore and tossing their crests of spray: the illustration here embraces not only the even onward march of each advancing rank, but also the moment of impact and the shock and commotion that will follow it. At the beginning of the third day's fighting (*Iliad* 11. 62 ff.) Hector as seen by the people on the other side is compared to the ominous dog-star (brightest star in the sky and ominous because associated with a season dangerous to health) appearing and disappearing among shifting clouds: here the comparison conveys simultaneously the glitter of Hector's helmet and armour, the menace that he represents, and the way he is glimpsed and lost to view and seen again among the mass of fighting men. In another passage (*Iliad* 15. 271 ff.) the triumphantly advancing Greeks are halted and afraid when Hector reappears in the battle, as hunter and hounds are checked in pursuit of a quarry when a lion appears and the hunted beast escapes: here hunters, quarry, and lion in the simile all correspond respectively to Greeks, Trojans, and Hector. In the *Odyssey* Odysseus, chilled and naked after his escape from shipwreck and sea, makes himself snug and warm under a blanket of leaves and the shelter of a thick bush (*Odyssey* 5. 488 ff.): he is compared to a glowing brand which a man on a remote farm buries in ashes so that it will stay aglow to make fire for him when he needs it—and here again each point in the simile illustrates something in the story: the loneliness of Odysseus, the protective nature of his covering, and the vital warmth that it protects.

Sometimes the correspondence between the simile and the point that it illustrates is less than exact. At Odysseus' first attempt at landing in Phaeacia after his shipwreck the skin is ripped from his fingers as the backwash of a wave drags him from the rock to which he has been clinging (*Odyssey* 5. 432 ff.). The comparison offered in this case is with a cuttlefish dragged from its lair, bringing away shingle still held by its tentacles. But the skin is ripped from Odysseus (not the rock) in the story, whereas in the illustration the shingle is ripped from the seabed (not the cuttlefish). Again, there is a passage in the *Iliad* (13. 491 ff.) in which Aeneas, calling on his men and glad to find them follow his call, is compared to a shepherd who is glad when he sees his sheep follow their ram to the place where he wishes them to water: here the shepherd is glad like Aeneas, and the sheep follow like Aeneas' men, but it is the ram they follow, not the shepherd. Odysseus, tossing sleepless and impatient as he waits for daybreak before the crisis of the Odyssey (20. 24 ff.), is compared to a man tossing and turning a sausage (more strictly, á paunch) as he cooks it, in a hurry to get it cooked: here it is the man who is impatient and the sausage that is turned and tossed, whereas in the story the impatience and the tossing and turning both pertain to Odysseus. Again, in the scene in the *Iliad* where Achilles, flame-lit, makes his dramatic appearance at the moat of the camp (then threatened by the Trojans' advance), the supernatural flame that crowns his head is compared (*Iliad* 18. 207 ff.) to a beacon lit by the defenders of a beleaguered town to summon aid from neighbouring allies: here the beacon corresponds to the supernatural flame and the beleaguered town corresponds to the menaced camp, but Achilles is bringing aid, not summoning it from others. In all these cases the felt effect of the simile is strong and clear, and it is unlikely that any ordinary reader is, or hearer was, troubled by the lack of exact correspondence. Indeed, analogies that embrace several points of comparison are rarely exact, least of all when they are produced impromptu, whether by invention or by an inspired adaptation of an item drawn from stock. That similes may be drawn from stock as well as freshly invented for their purpose appears from the fact that some are repeated in different contexts—the exultant stallion (of Paris at *Iliad* 6. 506 and Hector at *Iliad* 15. 263), the lion driven off from a farmstead and reluctantly departing (of Ajax at *Iliad* 11. 548 and Menelaus at *Iliad* 17. 657), the water trickling down a rock-face (of Agamemnon's tears at *Iliad* 9. 14 and Patroclus' at *Iliad* 16. 3).

Sometimes it seems clear that the poet's choice of an illustration has been influenced by conscious or subconscious awareness of something in the context other than the thing immediately being illustrated. The horses of Achilles, standing immobile with bowed heads in grief for Patroclus, are compared (*Iliad* 17. 434 ff.) to a tombstone with reference specifically to their immobility; but it is natural to suppose that it is the association of tombstones with death that has suggested the image, just as it does in fact enhance the value of it. More remarkable is the simile used to render the intensity of Odysseus' weeping as he hears the bard sing of his own exploits at the taking and sack of Troy: his tears are compared (*Odyssey* 8. 523 ff.) to the tears of the *victim* of a sack, a woman who is torn weeping from her dead husband's body to be led away prodded by the spears of her captors, to be a slave.

The similes then give impact, and sometimes additional significance, to particular moments of the story. They also, because of the variety and elaboration of the scenes they introduce, add a purely decorative element to its texture, like the incidental details—flowers and small animals and distant views of common human activities—

that appear in mediaeval and renaissance paintings without apparent relevance to the principal subject. In them especially—and this applies to both their functions—appears the sympathy of the poet's eye and ear with our own experience that wakes a response of quick recognition, and makes his story real. He and we are very far apart in time, but we feel no separation of experience between us when he speaks of the swarming of flies around milk-pails in the summer, the scattering of a chaff-heap by a puff of wind, waves moving shoreward in an endless succession of long ranks, the blanketing of vision in a thick fog, the slow succession of clear drops from melting snow, the curious impression received as we watch a chemical reaction (in this case, curdling), a poppy's head on its long stalk, a child tumbling a sand-castle, the immovability of a stubborn animal, the sulphurous smell following an electrical discharge, a bright star appearing and disappearing among broken cloud, the elastic agility of a flipped bean, the uncanny sensation of frustrated flight and pursuit in a dream, the hiss and seething of water when a hot object is plunged into it, the sight of a catch of fishes piled on a quayside, the mysteriously silent speed of falling snow-flakes in a blizzard, of a shooting star, of a swooping falcon.

This ends our catalogue of Homeric ways and means. It remains to draw the several threads together.

CONCLUSION

In *Iliad* and *Odyssey* alike are found:

A story with an important and representative human experience at its heart brought through a succession of moving incidents to a strongly moving conclusion.

A fragmented panorama of the world in which the stories unfold, glimpsed parenthetically (as it were) in similes and ornamental epithets and recurrent descriptions of events recurrent in life itself.

An organic unity of design, given by a governing theme which is complete, compact and clear in its outline, and which binds together the several parts of the whole in a functional relationship to itself.

A narrative element which is lucid (because conveyed in simply and orderly constructed language), and vivid (because concentrated on visible and audible particulars), and rapid (because selective of the moments on which it dwells). And a dramatic element of direct speech which can render every variety of emotional tone and personal style.

A flow of sound and rhythm which is swift (because predominantly dactylic), effortless (because derived from a habit of impromptu composition and oral delivery), abundantly varied, sometimes expressive, and always positively interesting and agreeable, within the discipline of a governing rhythm that is fixed and exact without being over-emphatic.

A diction which is unprosaic but also uncontrived; which is distinctively but not artificially mannered; and which commands (but expends with economy) a large vocabulary of expressive words and a large supply of artifices of arrangement.

And, finally, a persistent appeal, directed no doubt by instinct rather than conscious design, to timeless and universal human experience, which wakes the hearer's or reader's imagination to supply what the poet has felt but left unsaid.

The method of presentation varies naturally with the subject matter. Some passages are full of strong words and resonant sounds—passages descriptive, for instance, of vehement action or majestic pageantry, or expressive of violent passion or elegiac pathos. In other passages, and they are many, the attraction is simply that of clear narrative in a satisfying but unostentatious metrical and linguistic dress. And in others again a few significant effects of sound and metre are secondary to the strong impact of the narrated incidents themselves.

Illustration of the first of these varieties is hardly possible in English. Illustration of the second is unnecessary. A translation may go some way to illustrate the third. The two passages which follow may serve this purpose, and also bring this essay to an end.

The first of these passages is from the *Odyssey* (21. 392–430), and describes Odysseus' stringing of the bow, as immediate prelude to the destruction of the suitors. One of the two loyal servants to whom Odysseus has disclosed himself has gone out of the hall to make fast the courtyard gates. This done, he now returns.

> Then he went back into the hall and sat down again in the seat which he had left; and he kept his eyes fixed on Odysseus. Odysseus now had the great bow in his hands and was turning it this way and that, to see that worm had not eaten into the horn (of the stave) while its master was away. And a suitor said, turning to the man beside him: 'One would think him a fancier of bows

or some kind of expert, or maybe he has one like that himself at home, or is minded to make one, that wretched beggar—to see the way he turns it to and fro.' And another insolent young fellow said: 'I surely wish that man may be as lucky as he's likely ever to be able to string that bow.' So spoke the suitors. But when Odysseus, man of many wiles, had done with handling the bow and looking it over—easily then as a singer practised with the lyre will stretch a string over a new peg, fastening the twisted sheep-gut at either end, even so without effort did Odysseus string the mighty bow. And he held it with his right hand, and tried the string: and it sang out sweetly, clear as a swallow's note. The suitors were struck aghast; and all turned pale; and Zeus thundered aloud, showing a sign. Glad then was the lord Odysseus, man much tried, because the subtle counsellor Cronos' son sent him that sign. And he took a swift arrow that lay beside him on the table, ready: the rest were stored still in the hollow quiver: soon the Achaeans were to come to know them. Odysseus set the arrow to the bow-stave, and he drew the bowstring taut, and the notches with it, seated as he was, not moving from his chair; and he aimed and shot, and did not miss: the bronze-shod arrow flew through all the axes, over the ends of their hafts, and away beyond. Then Odysseus turned to Telemachus and said: 'Telemachus, the guest who sits in your hall has not disgraced you. I did not miss my mark, nor labour long in bending of the bow: my strength is still as it was of old, not as the suitors think, who insult and scorn me. And now is time for the Achaeans' supper also to be served them, in daylight; and then for another kind of sport to follow, with dance and song and music of the lyre: for these are the adornments of the feast.'

The language of this passage in the original exhibits the variety of rhythm and the inconspicuous assonances that are general character-istics of Homeric verse. And, more specifically, it assists by effects of metre and word-sound the descriptions of the effortless stringing of the lyre, and the musical twang of the bowstring, and the dark allusions to the impending destruction of the suitors. It also assists, by a managed relationship of the syntax to the metre, the later account of the process of drawing and discharging the bow and of the triumphant flight (not quite instantaneous but, for a brief moment, watched) of the straight-shot arrow.

But essentially the effect of the episode comes from the character of the particulars which the narrator has chosen to report. When he makes the servant at the beginning fix his eyes upon Odysseus, he invites his audience (ourselves) to do the same. And then, because the postures and movements (and sounds) reported have each a positive and therefore easily imaginable quality, we do in fact seem to see and hear each movement of the action that then follows.

All of this is vivid. Some of it is expressive too of something not directly stated—of Odysseus' mastery of the situation and his confident and effortless superiority. And a good many readers will feel a special and additional effectiveness in the opening tableau, of Odysseus turning the bow this way and that to inspect it, while the suitors watch and comment. For this will awake an echo in the common experience of most of us, the quite distinctive sensation of expectancy that is aroused in witnessing the careful examination of an object or a promised attempt at some exacting feat. The result is to communicate the atmosphere of tension in the hall, which the poet feels no need to describe directly; and also to quicken our sensitivity to all the scene that follows.

The second promised example is from the *Iliad* (22. 437-72) and tells how Andromache learns of Hector's death. After what has been said above it will require no separate commentary, for the method in essence is the same as in the passage quoted above.

But Hector's wife meanwhile knew none of this; for no true messenger had come to tell her that her husband stayed outside the gates. She was working her loom at the end of the great hall, weaving a piece of double width, purple and intricately patterned. And she called to the women with braided hair who served her in the house, bidding them set the great cauldron on the fire, to have warm water ready for Hector's bath when he should come home from the battle—all unsuspecting that no baths were now for him, whom bright-eyed Athena had struck down by Achilles' hand. Then she heard the sound of wailing and lamentation from the wall; and she trembled all over and let fall her shuttle to the ground; and she spoke again to the women with braided hair who served her, saying: 'Come with me, two of you: I must see what it is that has happened. I heard my husband's honoured mother's voice; and my heart in my breast beats fast and chokes me, and my knees beneath me are gone numb. Far from my hearing be the thought I utter: but I have a dreadful fear lest the lord Achilles cut off brave Hector from his friends, and drive him away from the city to the plain, and quench that fatal courage that was always his—for never would he keep his place among the rest, but must always run far out ahead, yielding to none in fire and courage.' So saying she rushed through the hall and away, like a woman possessed, with pounding heart: and her maids went with her. And when she came to the wall and the men that were gathered there, she stood at the parapet, and there out on the plain she saw him being dragged along: and the swift horses were dragging him pitilessly to the hollow ships of the Achaeans. Black night darkened her eyes, and she fell backward, and gasped, and fainted; and her shining head-dress fell far from her head, circlet and coif and woven band, and the veil that golden Aphrodite gave her on the day when Hector of the glittering helmet brought her home as his bride from Eëtion's house, having given gifts unnumbered.

POSTSCRIPT

This essay has described itself as an Introduction to Homer, and it does not pretend to be more than that. It has been concerned with the nature of Homeric poetry and the reasons, or some of them, for the power of its impact upon the reader. It has not attempted to discuss the varieties of special significance, representative or symbolic or allegorical, which many admirers have found in the stories told or in particular scenes or figures that appear in them. This is not because such responses to the poet's art are without validity, but because they are of necessity personal, products not of the poetry alone but of the encounter of this with the respondent's temperament and experience, time and place, and cultural and educational background. The study of them would be the task of a book of different intention and wider scope than this one. Some brief remarks that seem to one reader at least to come near to the heart of the matter will be found in Paul Mazon's final chapter in the Budé Introduction to the Iliad, and in the first of G.M. Sargeaunt's collected essays on Classical subjects — a work by now, alas, not easy to procure.[55]

NOTES

1a. From the fourth century BC onward the ancients understood by 'Homer' the author of the *Iliad* and *Odyssey*. Earlier, other epics too, now lost, were ascribed to 'Homer', perhaps at one time all ancient epic songs.

1b. There were many contenders in ancient times for the honour of being Homer's birthplace. The names of seven of them were put together to make, in Greek or Latin, a hexameter verse: *Smyrna, Rhodos, Colophon, Salamis, Chios, Argos, Athenae.*

1c. That iron was familiar to the maker of the poems appears from fairly frequent and significant references—about thirty in all. E.g.: there is a wood-cutter's axe of iron (*Iliad* 4. 485); ten axes of iron offered by Achilles as a prize in the games at Patroclus' funeral (*Iliad* 23. 851); twelve axes of iron set up for the bow-test in the Odyssey (*Odyssey* 19. 574 and 21. 97, etc.); the process of tempering an iron axe by sudden cooling, in a simile (*Odyssey* 9. 393). There is an iron arrowhead (*Iliad* 4. 123); knives or daggers of iron (*Iliad* 18. 34 and 23. 30); an iron mace (*Iliad* 7. 141). There is an iron chariot-axle (*Iliad* 5. 723). The gates of Tartarus are of iron (*Iliad* 8. 15). There is a big ingot of iron offered as a prize at the games for Patroclus (*Iliad* 23. 834); and the pretended trader Mentes (= Athena in disguise) is carrying a cargo of iron (*Odyssey* 1. 184). As an epithet 'iron' is applied metaphorically to irresistible force (*Iliad* 23. 177, of fire) and impenetrable hardness (*Iliad* 4. 510, of invulnerability); and to hardness of heart (*Odyssey* 5. 191 and *Iliad* 22. 357 etc.), and dauntless courage (*Iliad* 24. 205); and to the din of armed conflict (*Iliad* 17. 424). Finally, 'iron' is used by an evidently familiar trope for 'weapons' generally, in the excuse that Odysseus proposes his son should give for removing the arms from the hall when the attack on the suitors is being planned (*Odyssey* 16. 294 and 19. 13).

The otherwise consistent appearance of bronze as material for weapons throughout the poems seems to be due to the preservative power of a poetic phraseology which became traditional because of its convenience for impromptu composition in metre, and thus ensured the survival in poetry of a picture of conditions that were long since past in real life. For instance the phrase 'with the pitiless bronze' (*nēleï chalkō*) occurs more than fifteen times at line-ends; 'with the sharp bronze' (*oxeï chalkō*) occurs more than thirty times in the same position; 'brazen spear' (*chalkeon enchos*) more than twenty times; and so on. The effect of this accords well, of course, with the poet's purpose to evoke an heroic past: the men who fight with bronze are men 'not such as men now are'.

2. An author generally believed to be of the fourth century BC makes an Athenian say, in an imaginary dialogue, that 'Hipparchus was first to bring the poems of Homer to this land; and he ordained that the professional reciters at the Panathenaic Festival should recite them, taking turns, in continuous sequence, as still they do today' (*Platonic Corpus* 228 B). Hipparchus was one of the Pisistratid family who ruled Athens from 560 to 510 BC. A story later retailed by Cicero (*de Oratore* 3.137) that Pisistratus himself was 'said to have set out the poems of Homer as we have them, after they had previously been in confusion' may well be a garbled derivative of the same story that is told of Hipparchus above; it anyway agrees in carrying back the knowledge of the *Iliad* and *Odyssey* at Athens as far as the sixth century BC.

3. A *terminus ante quem* for the making of the poems is difficult to fix. It seems natural, considering the obscurity that surrounds the authorship of their creation, to suppose that it was earlier in time than the appearance of personal poetry and personally identified poets in the seventh century BC. But though epic poetry certainly existed before then, this does not enable us to assume the same of the special development of epic poetry which the *Iliad* and *Odyssey* represent. And if the maker of them (or of either of them, if with some critics ancient and modern we think that they had two separate authors) was not an isolated individual, but an exceptionally gifted member of a possibly numerous class or group of epic singers, it could well happen that his individuality did not at first stand out; the story-telling poet does not, like the author of personal poetry, give information about himself. As for occurrences in seventh-century poets of phrases that occur also in *Iliad* or *Odyssey*, these could be echoes in both contexts from epic songs that were older than them both. Thus, a date as late

as the sixth century BC for the creation of the Homeric poems cannot be regarded as an impossibility. Thespis, the titular father of tragic drama, is a hardly less shadowy figure than Homer: yet he is recorded as winning a prize at Athens in or about 534 *BC*

However, the opinion of most of those best qualified to judge puts the making of the *Iliad* near the end of the eighth century, and the making of the *Odyssey* perhaps a little later.

4. An example often quoted, and easily accessible, is the *Song of Roland*: see for instance the Introduction to the translation in the Penguin Classics (1957) pp. 7–8.

5. See for instance Wace and Stubbings, *Companion to Homer*, pp. 385–6.

6. The extent of this tendency to 'symmetrical' arrangement is variously estimated by those who have studied it; but the fact of its presence in some degree is beyond dispute. Thus, the last event on the battlefield (*Iliad* 22) is the terrible combat between Achilles and Hector, watched by Priam and Hecuba from the city-wall above; while the first event on the battlefield (*Iliad* 3) is the abortive and semi-farcical combat between Menelaus and Paris, watched by Helen from the city-wall above. And curious scenes of a quite distinctively similar character to one another occur, lowering the tension, both in the first day's fighting (*Iliad* 5) and in the last (*Iliad* 20–1): in both the Trojan Aeneas is snatched away by a god from before a dangerous adversary; in both a hero (Glaucus in one case and Aeneas in the other) pauses in mid-battle to narrate a long genealogy to his opponent; in both the god Ares and the goddess Aphrodite join in the fighting and are rudely humiliated.

The account of the first day's fighting, which is of some length, itself exhibits a chiastically ordered repetition of motifs in its contents. It occupies five books (*Iliad* 3–7), but does not advance the development of the action, the 'purpose of Zeus' to bring about defeat of the Greeks being in abeyance until the beginning of Book 8. It consists of a loose assembly of episodes which all make a useful and intended contribution (introductory in its nature) to the total effect of the poem, but are themselves casually rather than logically motivated. Among them the following order can be observed:

> Single combat (Menelaus and Paris)
> Scene in Troy (Helen and Paris)
> Diomede and the Lycian Pandarus
> Diomede and the goddess Aphrodite
> Sarpedon the Lycian's wounding
> Diomede and the god Ares
> Diomede and the Lycian Glaucus
> Scene in Troy (Hector, Hecuba, Paris, Helen, Andromache)
> Single combat (Hector and Ajax)

The purpose of this collection of episodes, plainly enough, is to introduce the principal actors of the tragedy that is to follow, with Diomede on the Greek side taking the lead on this first day in place of Ajax who is to take it in the intenser struggle which is to follow on the third day in Books 11–15. Many of the individual scenes are excellent, and so is the collective effect. But the collection has been inserted here and composed internally without much regard for natural probability. For instance, Menelaus and Paris need not have involved their respective peoples in nine years of war, if they were prepared to settle their difference, as now appears, in single combat between themselves; nor will Priam naturally need to enquire of Helen, after nine years, who of his principal adversaries is who; nor, after the treacherous breach of truce that followed the duel between Menelaus and Paris, will a second cessation of hostilities for a second duel (between Hector and Ajax) be easily arranged on the same day. It seems that a 'symmetrical' principle of order has been adopted here in the absence of an order dictated by the logic of a developing story—the development of the story being here in abeyance, and the included episodes being here included to serve a different purpose. This may reflect an early, primitive, approach to the problem of grouping short episodes to form a larger whole. It may also have served originally as an aid to memory. In the *Odyssey*, where 'symmetry' of construction is not apparent (unless in the grouping of Odysseus' adventures in Books 9–12) it is noticeable that aids to memory are provided by predictions of what *will* happen at the beginning of Books 1 and 5 and the end of Book 13, and by retrospective summaries of what *has* happened in the narratives of Odysseus to his wife in Book 23 and of the dead suitor's ghost to Agamemnon's ghost in the underworld in Book 24: these between them make a complete précis of the contents of the poem.

7. Thus Diomede (*Iliad* 5. 302) hurls a great stone 'that two men such as men now are could not carry'. And Aeneas (20. 285) does the same. Ajax (12. 380) heaves high aloft and throws a stone 'that even a strong man in his prime, as men now are, could hardly hold up with both hands'. Hector (12. 445) takes up and throws a stone 'that two men of the best, as men now are, could hardly avail to lift onto a waggon'.

The heroes are still near to a race of divine ancestors; some are sons of gods or goddesses, some fight with gods in battle; many are described as peers of gods, or god-like to behold.

8. When Agamemnon early in the story pretends to advise his men to abandon the expedition, they eagerly assent and rush to launch their ships without delay (*Iliad* 2. 149). When Paris and Menelaus propose to settle the issue by fighting one another in single combat, both Greeks and Trojans are overjoyed (3. 111); and when the duel between the two is about to begin, the men on both sides pray to heaven that the beginner of the trouble may be the one to fall, and 'that peace and friendship may be for us henceforth' (3. 320 ff.). The Trojans, we are told, detest Paris as cause of their sufferings (3. 454); and the Trojan herald Idaeus names him with a curse when he comes to propose a truce at the end of the first day's fighting (7. 390). Zeus, king of the gods and father of gods and men, loathes and despises Ares the god of war (5. 890).

Nevertheless, the war is thought of fatalistically as a visitation sent by the gods on men, part of the inevitable sorrows to which mankind is subject: so Priam says to Helen (3. 164), and Achilles to Priam (24. 525 ff., 547), and Odysseus to Agamemnon (14. 85 ff.); and this too is the comment of King Alcinoüs to Odysseus in the *Odyssey* (8. 579 ff.), 'it was the gods that ordained it, dooming men to perish, to make a tale for poets in time to come.'

9. So to Alcinoüs (*Odyssey* 7. 216): 'for this wretched thing, the belly, is utterly relentless, and forces a man to heed it, even in distress and heaviness of heart'. And to Eumaeus (15. 344): 'no mortal is more miserable than a homeless wanderer, but misery men must suffer for the cursed belly's sake . . .'. And to Eumaeus again (17. 286): 'the call of the belly none can dissemble, the cursed belly that makes much misery for men'. And to the suitors (17. 474): 'no bitterness is there nor heartache when a man is stricken in fighting for his possessions . . . but Antinoüs struck me in my belly's cause, the cursed

belly that makes much misery for men'. And to the suitors again, on Irus' challenge (18. 53): 'an old man worn out with suffering stands no chance against a young man in a fight; but this rascal belly eggs me on, to get myself a hiding'. Compare too 17. 559; 18. 2, 364, 380. There is a special, if comical, appropriateness in the simile (6. 130 ff.) which compares the naked and hungry Odysseus to a lion made bold by the call of its belly, when he emerges from the undergrowth to confront the Phaeacian girls.

10. Contrast with the above *Iliad* 1. 503 ff. for instance, where Thetis speaks: 'Father Zeus, if ever among the immortals I did you good service by word or deed, grant this my earnest prayer: *honour* my son, who is doomed as no man else to early death, and now King Agamemnon has slighted his *honour*, taking away my son's prize for himself: but do you *honour* him, Olympian lord of counsel, and give the Trojans mastery until the Achaeans *honour* my son and pay him *honour* due'. And again Patroclus (16. 269 ff.): 'Be men, my friends, and bear yourselves as stout soldiers should, that we may *honour* Peleus' son who is best by far of all the Argives here beside the ships, he and his warrior squires, and that Atreus' son wide-ruling Agamemnon may know and rue his folly, that he paid no *honour* to the best of the Achaeans'.

11. The word for this respect is *aidōs*. Achilles fails first, as Ajax implies (*Iliad* 9. 640), in respect for the consideration due to guests under a man's roof and to the claims of friendship, when he rejects the amends offered and the appeal made to him after the first defeat of the Greeks. He fails again, as the god Apollo declares (24. 43), in respect for the claims of decency and mercy when he persists in maltreatment of Hector's body. Zeus later affirms the essential decency of Achilles' nature (24. 157), and this affirmation is justified in what follows.

   aidōs and its related verb are used in a fairly wide range of contexts, often of respect for hierarchy, authority and so on, but also of respect for public opinion, humanity, and consideration for a person's feelings—thus Telemachus (*Odyssey* 4. 326) asks Menelaus not to let pity or concern for his feelings (*aidōs*) prevent him from telling what he knows of Odysseus' fate even if the news is bad. *aidōs* inhibits ruthlessness, recklessness, arrogance and vulgarity: it is complement and counterweight to the heroic urge to excel (*aristeuein*). From the combination of the two proceeds the moral and material advance of human societies.

12. Besides the thoroughly humanized Olympian gods there appear vaguer personifications of powers with special functions: *Strife* and *Blind Folly* (which possess a man despite himself); *Prayers* (which are felt to put at risk those who disregard them); *Rumour* (which swells fast from small beginnings to become a mighty force). Different again from these personifications are the *Erinyes*, upholders of the sanctity attaching to the customary and natural order of things: they punish breaking of oaths (*Iliad* 19.259), and offences against parents (*Iliad* 9.454; *Odyssey* 2.135) or against elders (*Iliad* 15.204), and they stop the prophetic utterance of the horse Xanthus (*Iliad* 19.418) because human speech is not in nature a horse's prerogative.

13. The telling of a story by a character in the story is in itself quite a common feature of both the Homeric poems—Nestor and Phoenix and others tell stories in the *Iliad*, and Nestor and Menelaus and Eumaeus, and Odysseus himself repeatedly, do the same in the *Odyssey*. In the case of the story Odysseus tells in Alcinoüs' palace, which occupies four whole books (*Odyssey* 9–12), this familiar feature of epic narrative has been developed in an extraordinary way to become a structural device essential to, and distinctive of, the economy of the poem as a whole. As such it is productive of two evident advantages. It enables the whole of Odysseus' adventures since the fall of Troy to be brought in without losing the compactness of plot, so much admired by Aristotle (*Poetics* 26.14) in *Odyssey* and *Iliad* alike, which is achieved by taking the actual homecoming of Odysseus for subject of the poem. And it transfers the part of the story which takes place in fairyland (as it were) onto a clearly different plane from the part which takes place in the usually realistic setting of domestic life in Ithaca and Peloponnese. It will be noted also that the transition into and out of fairyland is elegantly accomplished. For an element of wonder begins to appear already in Menelaus' palace in Book 4, with Helen's magic potion and Menelaus' adventure with the old man of the sea. Calypso's island, next, and Phaeacia, which provides the setting in which Odysseus narrates his earlier experiences with giants and witch and monsters, are in a sort of halfway world between fairyland and reality. And when Odysseus is transported from Phaeacia to his home-land, he is in a deep sleep, from which he awakes as from a dream.

14. When Penelope sets the suitors the test of bow and axes it does not follow that she has decided to surrender, though she evidently risks having to do so and her demeanour (e.g. at *Odyssey* 20. 79 and 21. 55) accords with the knowledge of this. It is possible indeed that

she is convinced (rightly, as the event shows) that the test will defeat the suitors; but there is no indication that such is her belief in the story as we have it. As the story runs, it seems that she throws out (at 19. 570 ff.) a mention of her purpose respecting the test (whether firm or tentative or pretended at this point) with the idea of seeing how the stranger, to whom she is talking, responds. He has assured her that he knows Odysseus' return to be imminent, and though earlier disappointments have hardened her in scepticism, she has formed a good opinion of this informant's personal worth and has also tested his credibility in another matter. He now tells her firmly to set the test without delay, since Odysseus will be on the scene before any of the suitors passes it. She makes no comment on this but takes leave of him for the night. Next morning the immediate impulse to produce the bow and axes comes to her from the goddess Athena's prompting. (It is hard to be certain whether at 19.570 the Greek words mean 'the dawn of the evil day is drawing near when I shall leave Odysseus' house, for now I intend . . .', or 'tomorrow's dawn will bring the evil day when . . .'.)

It was the view of some readers in the ancient world (see for instance Seneca, *Epp.* 88.8) that Penelope has penetrated her husband's disguise already before the dénouement. An early recognition in the full sense seems excluded by her reactions to Eurycleia's report in Book 23; but one can imagine that an intuition has prepared her subconsciously for the truth. We are left free by the poet to make our own guesses.

15. This reconciliation was necessary to the peace of mind of the poet's hearers, because the kinsmen of the killed suitors would be under an obligation to exact retribution, as were the kinsmen of the men killed by Theoclymenus (15. 272–8). Since many leading families in Ithaca and the adjoining islands were involved, the result would have been an impossible situation. The poet has to invoke a *deus ex machina* to bring about the departure from normal practice which the reconciliation demands, and make it acceptable to the feelings of his audience. It is partly in preparation for this that Telemachus at the beginning of the story gives formal warning to the suitors to desist from their misdoings, with the express assertion that if they do not now desist their blood will be on their own heads (1. 374–80 and 2. 138–45).

16. Ancient commentators report that the Alexandrian scholars Aristophanes and Aristarchus (third and second centuries BC) con-

sidered *Odyssey* 23.296 ('and so they came to lie again in the marriage-bed that had been theirs of old') to be the 'end (*peras* or *telos*) of the *Odyssey*'. What they meant by this we do not know. They may have meant, what is certainly true, that with this line the end to which the plot has been leading—punishment of usurpers, reunion of husband and wife, and reinstatement of Odysseus in possession of his own home—is marked as achieved. All that follows in 23. 297 - 24. 548 is supplementary, a tying up of loose ends.

This supplementary material consists of (i) the tale told by Odysseus to Penelope of his past adventures; (ii) the arrival of the dead suitors' ghosts in the underworld and their meeting there with the ghosts of Achilles and Agamemnon; (iii) the reunion of Odysseus with his father Laertes, who has often been mentioned earlier in the story; (iv) the making of peace by Athena between Odysseus and the slain suitors' numerous and influential kinsmen.

The last two of these episodes are obviously indispensable in the circumstances. The first two are dispensable, but functionally valuable. The second, in bringing together in memory the destinies of Achilles and Agamemnon and Odysseus, furnishes both a final epilogue to the Tale of Troy and a reminder of the contrast between the homecomings of Agamemnon and Odysseus for which earlier references (in 1, 3, 4, 11) have prepared us, and which leads now in conclusion to a fitting eulogy of Odysseus' wife. Less aesthetically but still practically useful are the summary narratives of Odysseus to Penelope (23. 310–41) and of the dead suitor to Agamemnon (24. 121–90), which between them provide a complete table of contents of the preceding poem.

Occasional singularities of style and language in this part of the poem are more often apparent than real, and are susceptible anyway of various explanations. (One that perhaps deserves to be noticed is an unusual frequency of contracted forms and synizeses: 24. 323, 337, 339, 340, 341, 360, 381, 389, 394, 396, 398, 437, 485, 523, 534: one or two of these are unusual in themselves.)

17. Further discussion of the gods at this point would interrupt the progress of the essay's theme. Perhaps therefore a supplementary note of some length may be excused.

(1) The gods that help to people the Homeric world are often associated as protectors or possessors with particular places or peoples, or preside over particular functions, inhabiting such-and-such a locality or protecting such-and-such peoples or presiding over this or that activity. They also have affections and antipathies for individuals.

They have prerogatives that must not be infringed, and expectations of offerings and religious attentions which must not be neglected. Hence they have also a diversity of interests, and consequently of purposes. The result is that their operations are unco-ordinated and often in conflict with one another. In particular cases however it may be felt that a collective purpose prevails, or that one power stronger than the rest is imposing his will on the whole. There is also a feeling that some things are governed by a law superior even to the gods—for instance, that Sarpedon must fall by the hand of Patroclus, that Achilles' death must follow soon on Hector's, that Troy in the end must be taken and destroyed. The strongest of the gods, Zeus, is seen now as agent of this law, now as ordainer of it. These are different modes of *feeling* about the inevitable: we must not look in the Homeric world for an intellectually systematized theology.

(2) What is the relation of Homer's gods to the moral conduct of man to man? The answer seems to be that originally they are not concerned with it at all. The distinctive attributes of divinity are supernatural power and immortality; its distinctive concerns are with its own prerogatives; the gods punish offences against their own property and dependents. But the gods in various ways *become* concerned with the behaviour of man to man also. As ultimate power they are invoked in oaths to uphold the inviolability of contracts, and punish breaches of it. They are thought of too as having under their protection those whom human custom treats as entitled to compassion, such as suppliants and recipients of hospitality under a man's roof. Thus Agamemnon is sure that Zeus will not assist those who have broken the sworn truce (*Iliad* 4.235 ff.), and Menelaus is sure that Zeus as protector of guests will be angry with the Trojans who stole his wife and goods after enjoying his hospitality, and Hector believes the gods will be angry with Achilles for rejecting his plea for decent burial. And indeed the gods *are* angry when they look down and see the brutal way in which Achilles treats his victim's body. In fact, outside the special contexts of oaths and compacts made with gods for witness, there is a divine public opinion which operates much as does human public opinion, condemning certain sorts of bad behaviour, and more powerful than human opinion though also more remote and disinterested. But this is a matter of feeling, not of law. In the turbulent conditions that prevail in the *Iliad* this kind of divine concern is naturally not much in evidence, especially as the division of their sympathies between the warring parties hampers the emergence of any consensus among the gods themselves. In the more settled conditions that prevail in the

Odyssey the feeling is clear that the gods collectively care for justice among men; especially in the minds of humble people such as the swineherd, who seek protectors against oppression and turn naturally to whatever power is stronger than their oppressors, with hope and faith bred of hope. 'The gods do not approve of wicked deeds,' says Eumaeus 'they honour justice and righteousness in men' (*Odyssey* 14. 83–4); and indeed the whole story of the Odyssey is premised on the idea that the suitors are to be punished, under Athena's super-intendence, for their 'insolence and wickedness' which has moved the gods to indignation (23. 67). This indignation however is not different in kind from the indignation of the gods at Achilles' treat-ment of Hector's body in the *Iliad*; and Athena's concern is at least as much for her favourite Odysseus as for any general concept of right and justice. Where human indignation is acute enough, the gods are imagined as indignant too, and so as apt to use their power to punish. But the standard is set by man, not given him by the gods. And just as human disapproval of the unkindness of man to man is erratic and intermittent and only occasionally effective, so is the corresponding but remoter indignation of the gods.

(3) A further question relates to the comic, even farcical, treatment which the gods receive in some passages. The wounding of Ares and Aphrodite by Diomede, and their screams and undignified conduct thereafter (*Iliad* 5); the lubricious exploitation of her sex-appeal by Hera to distract the attention of her husband while his intentions are being frustrated by Poseidon on the battlefield (*Iliad* 14); the crude bullying of Artemis by Hera and the knockout blow dealt by Athena to Ares in the grotesque brawl of the immortals which precedes the grim dénouement of the human story of the *Iliad* (21); and finally the tale of Ares and Aphrodite trapped in bed together by Aphrodite's lawful husband which is offered as an entertainment by the bard Demodocus at the games of the Phaeacians in the *Odyssey* (8)—in all these scenes the gods are depicted as behaving in a way which by human standards is variously vulgar or brutal or ridiculous. The effect is to throw the dignity of the human participants into relief, with the consequence indicated epigrammatically in Longinus' comment (*On the Sublime* 9.7) that 'Homer seems in the *Iliad* to have made his men gods and his gods men'. This treatment does not imply any lack of respect for the power of the gods, still less any scepticism about their existence. The power of the gods and the consequences of offending them are things of which the poet and his audience and his characters are very plainly aware. But what displeases the gods is

failure to make them proper offerings or generally respect their prerogatives, not what is said about them. And what man respects in them,
originally, is not their moral quality but their power. Fearing them
for this, and envying them for their immunity from death and age,
he is pleased to see them in imagination being sometimes taken down a
peg.

(4) Another question concerns the relation between supernatural
influence and human responsibility. When Achilles is about to lift
his hand against Agamemnon, it is Athena who restrains him. When
Helen resists the summons of Aphrodite to Paris's bed, she is sternly
compelled to submit. Zeus puts fear in Ajax, when he wishes to turn
the battle in the Trojans' favour; Athena puts courage in Menelaus for
the fighting over Patroclus's body. Hera prompts Achilles to question
Calchas as to the cause of the plague; Athena prompts Pandarus to
shoot the arrow that breaks the truce; Apollo and Hera prompt Helenus
to suggest to Hector the challenge which leads to his duel with Ajax
(in the seventh book); Athena in the *Odyssey* inspires Penelope with
her unwonted whim to appear in the hall before the suitors, and later
moves her to bring out the bow and axes for the trial that leads to the
final crisis. The Trojans when advised wisely by Polydamas to retire
behind their walls after the reappearance of Achilles are besotted by
Athena so that they reject him and follow the contrary and fatal
advice of Hector instead. When Odysseus warns the friendly suitor
Amphinomus to go away before destruction falls on his associates
he is prevented by Athena from giving heed to the warning. Patroclus
forgets Achilles's instruction to turn back after he has driven the
enemy from the ships because 'the purpose of Zeus is too strong
for mortals to resist'. Priam comforts Helen with the assurance that
she is not the cause of his troubles but that it was the will of the gods
to bring the war upon him. It is not surprising then that Agamemnon
declares (*Iliad* 19.86) that he was not the cause of (or to blame for)
his conduct towards Achilles but that it was a supernatural influence,
Infatuation, and that Zeus and Fate are the cause; and later Achilles
accepts that but for this Zeus-sent Infatuation Agamemnon would
never have acted as he did, 'but Zeus it seems was minded that many
of the Achaeans should perish'. Yet it is plain that his men *have* been
blaming Agamemnon as the *cause* of their troubles, from his own words
here; and earlier (13. 108 ff.) Poseidon in his exhortation to the troops
has said that the *fault* is Agamemnon's and that the blame for their
defeat lies 'with the feebleness of the commander and the slackness
of the men'. And when Hector is about to face Achilles at the end he,

unlike Agamemnon, says nothing of any god's compulsion but simply that through *his own folly* he has been the undoing of his army (22. 104). Similarly in the *Odyssey* we are told repeatedly that Odysseus's men and the suitors both brought their doom on themselves 'by their own folly and presumption'. Nor would the displeasure of the gods over Achilles' brutality to Hector's body be intelligible if his behaviour had been prompted solely by themselves. It is clear therefore that though man's actions are sometimes seen as governed by a supernatural will, they are often also seen as prompted by his own self. And indeed in several passages a speaker asks himself precisely whether it has been the one or the other: Telemachus' companion, when Telemachus is uncertain how to address his hosts, tells him (*Odyssey* 3.26) that 'he will think of some things for himself and god will put others in his head'; and the herald Medon, asked by Penelope why Telemachus has set out for Pylos, replies (4.712) that he does not know 'whether it was a god or his own impulse that roused him to it'.

It is in accord with this that people in the story are shown going through a process of deliberation and reaching decisions which are a product of this process—Odysseus, when (in the eleventh book of the *Iliad*) he finds himself left alone by his retreating companions and surrounded by the enemy; Menelaus, when he fears to abandon the body of fallen Patroclus but also sees coming an opponent for whom he knows he is no match; Hector, as he wonders for a moment whether to throw himself on Achilles' mercy.

In these and many other instances it is the person's own character that is seen as determining his conduct. It is the character of Agamemnon that makes him treat Chryses with arrogance as he does at the beginning of the story of the *Iliad*; and it is Achilles' character that makes him choose honour and achievement before long life, and Odysseus' character that makes him prefer home and wife to the gift of immortality proffered to him by Calypso.

Human actions are thus seen as motivated sometimes by human character and choice, and sometimes again by supernatural purposes which may determine or override human inclinations. That the supernatural purpose, if exerted, will prevail is naturally understood. But it is not felt to be exerted on each and every occasion. On the other hand, it becomes easy in retrospect to view the failing of an individual as part of a mechanism that brings a divine plan to fulfilment; and this way of looking at things is helpful, as in the case of Agamemnon, to self-excuse.

18. The chronology of the *Iliad* is broadly as follows:

Book 1 occupies twenty-three days (of which nine—the duration of the plague—are indicated in a single line at 1.53, and eleven—the duration of Zeus' absence in Ethiopia—in a single line at 1.493). This opening section carries the story from Agamemnon's rebuff of Chryses to the promise of Zeus to Thetis that he will cause the Greeks to suffer defeat. It has for its most significant episode the quarrel of Achilles and Agamemnon.

Books 2–22, with 23. 1–58, occupy five days. These contain: the marching out of the armies and the first day of battle (2–7.380); a one-day truce (7.381–482); the second day of battle (8); the third day of battle, and Achilles' reaction to the death of Patroclus (11–18.238); Achilles' reconciliation with Agamemnon and the fourth and final day of battle (19–22, with 23.1–58).

Books 23.59—end and 24 occupy twenty-five days (of which eleven—the growing displeasure of the gods at the maltreatment of Hector's body—are indicated in a single line at 24.30, and nine—the preparations for Hector's funeral—in a single line at 24.784. This concluding section carries the story from the funeral of Patroclus to that of Hector, and has for its most significant episode the relenting of Achilles and release of Hector's body for burial.

The total number of days covered by the action is thus fifty-three; of which however forty are disposed of in four lines. The recurrent figures nine-and-eleven and eleven-and-nine in the opening and concluding sections obviously reflect a conventional phraseology. But without placing emphasis on this correspondence of artificial arithmetic one can see an instinct for symmetry in the time-pattern of the whole.

The chronology of the *Odyssey* is broadly as follows:

Books 1–4 comprise six days, and contain the story of Telemachus' doings from his 'wakening' by Athena at the start of the poem to the morning of the day after his arrival at Sparta; together with a glance at events in Ithaca during his absence (4.625–847). The story includes Telemachus' warning to the suitors (2), and his visit to Pylos and Sparta, with a halt at Pherae on his way between (3–4.485).

Books 5–12, with 13.1–92, comprise twenty-seven days (of which four days of raft-building pass in one line at 5.62 and seventeen days of uneventful sailing pass similarly in one line at 5.81). These books contain the story of Odysseus' doings from Calypso's consent to release him to his arrival on the shore of Ithaca at 13.92. The story includes voyage, storm and shipwreck (5), and the events of three days spent amont the Phaeacians (6-7; 8-13.17; and 13. 18-77). It is on the evening of the second of these that Odysseus tells of his past adventures since the fall of Troy.

Books 13.93-23.343 comprise six days, and carry the story from Odysseus' arrival in Ithaca to the destruction of the suitors and the reunion of Odysseus and Penelope. The first of the six days is occupied by his waking, meeting with Athena, and entertainment in Eumaeus' hut (13.93-14). Two further days are occupied by the return of Telemachus from Sparta (15, in which cf. 185-9); and a third by the meeting of father and son under Eumaeus' roof (15.495—end of 16). Then follow two days in Odysseus' house (17.1-23.343, with a night intervening in 20.1-90), in which a series of various events reaches a climax in the production of bow·and axes by Penelope, the killing of the suitors, and the happy reunion of long-absent husband and long-suffering wife.

Book 23.343-72 and Book 24 dispose, in one day, of certain subsidiary but still important matters: a conclusion to the comparison earlier introduced between the fortunes of Agamemnon and Odysseus; reunion of Odysseus with his father, who though not participant in the action hitherto has been mentioned often in the story as living; and a reconciliation which will prevent the blood-feuds that else must have been a consequence of the killing of the suitors.

The action of the poem is thus completed in forty days, of which twenty-one are made to pass in two lines only. On the other hand the device of Odysseus' retrospective narrative to the Phaeacians enables the events of several years to be included.

19. It is not by an intrusion of modern sentiment that the affection of Penelope for Odysseus is seen as matched by his for her. At the beginning of the poem we are shown Odysseus 'longing for home and wife' (1.13). At the end he weeps as he holds 'his dear, true wife' in his arms (23.232 ff.). Calypso with a touch of jealousy speaks to him of his wife 'for whom you yearn day in day out' (5.40). He tells Nausicaa (6.182 ff.) that there is no better or greater blessing in the world 'than when man and wife keep house together, one in heart and mind'. The Phaeacian Euryalus in his apology to Odysseus prays that the gods may grant him 'to come home to your own land and see your wife again' (8.410). And his own prayer at parting from the Phaeacians (13.42 ff.) is 'that I may find at home my peerless wife

(or, my wife still true) and all my dear ones safe and sound'.

20. The quality of the poetry itself is really sufficient proof of a precedent tradition; and representatives of the bearers of such a tradition appear in the *Odyssey* in the persons of Phemius, the bard in Odysseus' household, and Demodocus in that of the Phaeacian king. They have extensive repertories, and from these they select subjects which have a certain resemblance to those of our *Iliad* and *Odyssey*: a Quarrel of Heroes, and the Homecoming of the Greeks from Troy. They sing impromptu; and one boasts that he is creative (*Odyssey* 22.347), implying that the accomplishment of others may be more narrowly repetitive of learned material.

Some particular items of internal evidence may be mentioned here: much fuller evidence is available in M. P. Nilsson, *Homer and Mycenae* (1933) and G. S. Kirk, *The Songs of Homer* (1962).

(1) The mixture of forms in the Homeric language (see text, p. 41) was obviously not a single man's improvisation—it would strike a hearer in that circumstance as grotesque. It must have developed over a period of time and (given its very evident metrical utility) in the context of metrical composition.

(2) The familiar recurrent phrases (see text, pp. 44–7) include some whose peculiar treatment reflects a traditionally stereotyped habit in the use of them. For instance, the genitive phrase *Achaiōn chalkochitōnōn* (= 'of the bronze-mailed Achaens': see p. 99 below on the pronunciation of the Greek) occurs at line ends no less than twenty-four times; while the no less metrically and syntactically convenient nominative *Achaioi chalkochitōnes* never occurs at all—the Achaeans in the nominative in that position being 'well-greaved' or 'warlike breed'. Again, some phrases can be seen to have entered the poetic vocabulary at different stages of its development. The accusative phrase *meliēdea oinon* ('honey-sweet wine') was coined—as the absence of elision between the two words shows—when *oinon* (the Latin *uinum*) had an initial sound (the digamma, pronounced like our w) which was later lost; while the corresponding genitive *meliēdeos oinou* was coined at a later time when the loss of the initial sound had already taken place.

(3) The poetic tradition, with its metrical habits, has preserved the use of bronze weapons in an iron-age poem (see note 1c. on pp. 65–6). This preservative effect is nicely illustrated by a report quoted by Milman Parry (*Harvard Studies* 43 (1932), 11) from an earlier work by A. Rambaud concerning the epic singers of a people in Russia

who had changed their landscape by migration long before: 'He (the bard) continues to sing of "stout oaks"—though he has never seen an oak in his life . . . he talks of "helms" and "iron maces" though he has no idea what these arms may be . . .' The man-length shield which appears (together with shields of quite other kinds) in the *Iliad*—knocking against Hector's neck and ankles as he goes from the battle-field with shield slung behind him at 6.117, or tripping Periphetes on its rim at 15.645—is otherwise known to us only from relics of the middle of the second millennium BC (beautifully illustrated on an inlaid dagger-blade from Mycenae in Nilsson, *Homer and Mycenae* facing p. 139, and see also p. 144). It is hardly conceivable that the maker of the *Iliad* can ever have seen such a shield. Yet when he mentions it, it is in terms that present a picture to the mind's eye.

21. The memory is a powerful and flexible engine in a mind not clogged by the complicated requirements of 'civilized' life, and not spoiled by the habit of reliance on writing. Much to the point here is Plato's fable (*Phaedrus* 274) about the invention of the art of writing by the legendary Theuth, and his conversation on the subject with the king of Egypt: 'When they came to the letters, Theuth began: "This invention, O king, will make the Egyptians wiser, and better able to remember, it being a medicine which I have discovered both for memory and wisdom." The king replied: "Most ingenious Theuth, one man is capable of giving birth to an art, another of estimating the amount of good or harm it will do to those who are intended to use it. And so now you, as being the father of letters, have ascribed to them, in your fondness, exactly the reverse of their real effects. For this invention of yours will produce forgetfulness in the minds of those who learn it, by causing them to neglect their memory, inasmuch as, from their confidence in writing, they will recollect by the external aid of foreign symbols, and not by the internal use of their own faculties. Your discovery, therefore, is a medicine not for memory, but for recollection—for recalling to, not for keeping in mind. And you are providing for your disciples a show of wisdom without the reality. For, acquiring by your means much information unaided by instruction, they will appear to possess much knowledge, while, in fact, they will, for the most part, know nothing at all; and, moreover, be disagreeable people to deal with, as having become wise in their own conceit, instead of truly wise."' (tr. J. Wright.)

Imagine now a man of extraordinary talent, and moreover a specialist (like enough) whose whole business in life is telling stories in epic verse, and hearing stories hold by other members of his profession. He has at his disposal a vocabulary and phraseology well suited to assist impromptu versification; he may of course also rehearse sometimes before performance. He knows about mnemonic devices to keep the sequence of his tales in order. His compositions can remain, and doubtless do remain, fluid in their particulars and subject to revision in their outlines until the point when by his death or for other reason they pass out of his control. If after that happens they are handed on by memory for some time before being fixed in writing, they will certainly be subject to accidental variations of detail, and perhaps of course to some wilful alterations also.

Writing with a serviceable alphabet, an early version of that used in the classical period, appears in Greece (as far as we know) in the first half of the eigth century BC. Writing materials convenient for literary composition—papyrus and (probably) reed pens—are thought to have first become available in the late seventh century; but they can hardly have been helpful for any but very limited purposes. Moreover the script used consisted of capital letters exclusively, without punctuation and without spacing between words; and the form of a document of any length was a roll, not inconvenient for continuous reading, but very inconvenient for reference. In due course—we believe before the end of the sixth century—it was found possible to commit the 28,000 odd lines of the *Iliad* and *Odyssey* to writing, in the script described, on a number of such rolls. The number required will have been very considerable, and the task itself arduous in the extreme. That such equipment can have been of any help for the *composition* of the poems is hardly possible to believe.

22. Numerous medieval manuscripts of the *Iliad* and *Odyssey* (more for the former than for the latter) present us with what is in all but details a uniform text; and since they are all of Byzantine origin or derived from Byzantine originals they can be taken to represent the standard 'Homer' current at Constantinople in, say, the year AD 1000. Fortunately, a very considerable number of papyrus fragments, ranging in date from the second century BC to the third century AD and beyond, enable a picture to be formed of the version current at that much earlier time; and this proves to correspond with the standard Byzantine version that we have.

About the middle of the second century BC a celebrated commentary on the poems was made by the then head of the great Library at Alexandria, Aristarchus. This event seems to have ensured the prevalence from that time on of a standard text of Homer, the one that we still have.

Before the middle of the second century BC our evidence is somewhat confused. The not very numerous papyrus fragments surviving from the third and early second centuries BC exhibit in some cases 'longer' versions—that is to say, versions with extra lines not now included in the text we know. These extra lines are not important, nor are important variations of any other kind observed in the 'longer' texts. Quotations in authors of the fourth and third centuries also depart sometimes from the text we know. This may be due sometimes to errors of memory; it may be due also to the spread of variant texts which had come into being with the growth of a book-trade— books being then reproduced by manual copying—or through the vagaries of itinerant reciters. Nevertheless, from the fifth century onward authors such as Thucydides, Plato, Xenophon, Aristotle, etc. refer to the Homeric poems in terms that assume that they are works whose content is common knowledge and that verbatim quotations moreover will be recognized by an ordinarily cultured man. Moreover, there is evidence (see p. 66 above) to support the belief that from the latter part of the sixth century BC a continuous recitation of the *Iliad* and *Odyssey* was an officially regulated feature of the Great Panathenaic Festival which was held at Athens every four years. This institution can be expected to have encouraged the preservation of a standard version of the poems. The observed influence of Attic dialect on the text we have may indeed indicate that a version preserved at Athens was its parent; though this influence could also be due to the fact that the Attic dialect was the basis of the all-purpose brand of Greek that spread as a lingua franca over the Eastern Mediterranean from the fourth century BC, and must have had its effect on the wording in reproduction of such universally popular but linguistically antiquated works as the Homeric poems.

There are uncertainties in all the above, but they are not such as need prevent its acceptance as a fair hypothesis. What remains wholly obscure is the mode of transmission and the length of its period, if any, which intervened between the making of the poems and the latter half of the sixth century.

23. For the fact that the Catalogue differs from the rest of the *Iliad* in its view of the principalities of the various chiefs see D. L. Page, *History and the Homeric Iliad* (1959), as modified by R. Hope Simpson and J. F. Lazenby in *The Catalogue of the Ships in the Homeric*

Iliad (1970). Moreover it not only reckons the units of the marching army in terms of ships, but also describes these as ships in motion (*neës kion, neës estichoönto* at 509, 516, 602, 680, 733, etc.). The poet names Protesilaus (698) as leader of the men from Phylace, but adds that he had been killed ten years before. He names Philoctetes (718) as leader of the men of Meliboea, but adds that he was actually not there at all but marooned on Lemnos. He lists the contingent of Achilles from Phthia (681 ff.) among the forces mustering for battle, but adds that in fact they were not there because Achilles had withdrawn them from service. It is thus clear that the Catalogue was not made for the place it now occupies in the *Iliad*. It is clear also that it derives ultimately from a record—surely poetical—of great antiquity, since the elaborate picture that it presents is a picture of Greece before the Dorian invasion of *c*. 1000 BC: there are no Dorians in the Catalogue. What changes of language and content the original underwent before our poet of the *Iliad* incorporated it in his great poem we cannot know, nor how much he contributed of his own in either respect.

But in the aesthetic design of the poem the Catalogue is integral. The poet's judgement in this respect set an example followed by (for example) Virgil in the *Aeneid* (7. 641 ff., the Italian tribes), and Milton in *Paradise Lost* (1. 376 ff., the fallen Angels), and Herodotus in his *Histories* (7. 61–99, the national contingents in Xerxes' army) and even Thucydides (7. 57-58, the opposed forces before the last sea-battle at Syracuse; also the elaborate catalogue of Sicilian peoples in 6. 1-5).

24. At *Iliad* 9.168 Nestor recommends that the deputation to Achilles should consist of Phoenix (to lead the way) and then Ajax and Odysseus, accompanied by two heralds. This is agreed. And when Odysseus presents Agamemnon's offer of amends to Achilles at 225 ff., Phoenix is present (223), as he is in all the rest of the scene in Achilles' hut, where Achilles detains him at the end (617, 658 ff.) in terms which ·show that he is conceived as having arrived as a visitor with the others. But in the account of the envoys' walk to Achilles' quarters (182 ff.), and their entry into his presence (when Odysseus is said, at 192, to lead the way) and his reception of them, there is no mention of Phoenix and only the dual number is used. This might indeed result from an economical use of stock phrases and an economical avoidance of dispensable detail. But it seems very possible that it results from incomplete reworking of an episode in which Phoenix was not originally present.

25. Odysseus describes his native island to the Phaeacians, as our poem has it, thus (*Odyssey* 9.21 ff.): 'My home is sunny Ithaca. It has in it a height called Neriton, wooded and wind-stirred, visible from far away. And round about are many islands set very close to one another, Dulichium and Same and forest-clad Zacynthus. Itself it is low, and lies furthest out to sea towards the darkness (? the west), while the rest are apart towards the dawn (? the east) and the sun.' The list of named islands, a stock line, recurs in the poem, at 1.246, 16.123, 19.131; and cf. also 16.247-51. It is generally assumed that Zacynthus and Ithaca were the islands known by those names in classical times, and that Same was an ancient name for Cephallenia, the big island that lies west of Ithaca and is divided from it by a narrow strait. Dulichium has presented a problem, for it furnished fifty-two suitors—the largest contingent—and there is no substantial island in the area additional to those listed above. It is usually and plausibly identified with Leucas, which strictly is a peninsula but comes very near indeed to being an island, as a map will show. But there is a worse puzzle to come: for classical and modern Ithaca is by no means 'low', having peaks of over 2,000 feet and a continuously hilly coastline. Nor is it by any means 'furthest out to sea' in relation to the other islands named, which form, broadly speaking, an arc to seaward of it. Various expedients (some reviewed in *Companion to Homer*, pp. 399 ff.) have been suggested to reconcile the statement in our *Odyssey* with the facts of geography; but the simplest supposition is that the position of Ithaca in relation to its neighbours has been mistaken by the maker of the *Odyssey*, or that an account once correct has been garbled in transmission. This is not incompatible with the fact that the maker of the poem appears to have been well informed concerning the position of Ithaca in relation to the *mainland* of Greece and the *presence* of a group of islands in its neighbourhood. The phrase 'itself it is low' occurs also in the description of Circe's island (10.196), and might be an intrusive echo from that passage or elsewhere.

26. The situation in the scene beginning at *Odyssey* 23.171 is that Penelope has at first been baffled by the unkempt and prematurely aged appearance (so contrived by Athena to prevent his earlier recognition) of the man who has killed the suitors and has then—after keeping his identity concealed from her during their long conversation the night before—been announced to be her husband. But Athena has meanwhile made him young and handsome again, and Penelope

has spoken to him in terms that imply recognition (175–6–'I know well how you looked when you took ship for Troy'). She now turns to Eurycleia and tells her, as our story runs, to make up a bed (or his bed) for him outside (178) the bedchamber that her master himself with his own hands built long ago; there Eurycleia is to put out (179) the bed and lay the bedding on it. Penelope here is, as we later learn (206, 225) making a final test of the identity of the man before her. But her instruction as it stands is either meaningless nonsense or an offensive rebuff to a husband come home at last. In neither case is it useful as a test, for an indignant reaction to the rebuff may come with equal probability from an indignant husband or a man pretending to be one.

Odysseus' reaction is indeed indignant; not however because he sees a rebuff in Penelope's words, but because he sees an implication of quite another kind. 'Who' he says 'has put my bed in another place?' And he goes on to explain that the bed in the bedchamber he built himself was so fixed that only an act of drastic interference could remove it. If therefore the bed *has* been 'put in another place', he will want an explanation.

Odysseus' reaction 'who has put my bed in another place?' would normally be elicited by one suggestion only—namely, that the bed should be put now in the place where he knows it ought already to be. And this is the reaction which Penelope must want to be sure of provoking (or not provoking, if the man she has before her is an impostor).

So that we can deduce that what Penelope really said to Eurycleia was 'put and make up his bed (or a bed) *in* the bedchamber that he built himself'; and that 'inside' has got changed to 'outside' in the process of transmission by someone who thought that 'put the bed out' (179) meant outside the bedchamber, whereas it can equally well refer to taking a bed outside the house to the bedchamber which (as we discover, 190) was built outside its main building, in the courtyard.

By saying 'put and prepare a bed for him in the bedchamber he built himself' Penelope sets a perfect test; for this is their bridal chamber (225 ff.), and Odysseus alone of all men will know that in the welcoming words there is something amiss.

27. The Visit to the Underworld (*Odyssey* 11) disturbs an otherwise clear—and therefore probably original—symmetry in the disposition of the adventures narrated by the hero: the threefold repetition of a series consisting of two briefer episodes followed by a long one

to be patient for a year longer and put up if need be with the wasting
of his substance. If on the other hand he hears that his father is dead,
he is to make a symbolic funeral for Odysseus, and proceed to arrange
for Penelope's remarriage. (The fact of her widowhood will then be
certain, and Telemachus will be head of the household.)

In this there is nothing to make the reader stumble. It is indeed
assumed by implication in the third injunction that Penelope will *not*
have returned to her father's house and sought a new marriage while
she still hopes for her husband's return, and that the suitors will *not*
forthwith depart on being given notice by Telemachus to do so. But
these assumptions accord with all that happens in the story and with
all that Telemachus and the audience are likely to expect.

Athena finally adds a further injunction: that after all the above
Telemachus is to 'take thought how to kill the suitors in the house,
by guile or openly', thus emulating the manly conduct of young Orestes
who killed his father's murderer Aegisthus. This seems to assume that
the suitors or some of them will continue to infest the house even after
Penelope has taken a new husband. This is quite compatible with what
we learn in the poem of the suitors and their mixed motives; and it is
necessary to the exhortation which makes the climax of Athena's
speech and which would be much weakened by the addition of a
conditional clause ('kill them, if they still won't go away'). But it is
an assumption less obviously natural than those earlier required.

Some find this speech of Athena easy to understand, economically
expressed, and well suited to the speaker's purpose; noting further
that as Telemachus will not in fact (in the story that follows) learn
that his father is dead there is no call for precision in imagining what
is to happen on the contrary supposition. Others on the other hand
feel that the absence of conditional clauses, in the last injunction
especially, makes the speech as it stands incoherent to a degree that
can only be explained by supposing that an originally intelligible
version has been confused by later reworking or interpolation, whether
by the first author or by another.

It will be seen that in this matter too there is no dogma to be revered, and every reader can safely form his own judgement for himself.

30. The appeal to the visual imagination—the mind's eye—appears
in a special form in the emphasis given by descriptions of various kinds
at the beginningof an important phase of action. The description may
be of a scene—of Achilles in his hut when the envoys come to him
in *Iliad* 9, and again when Priam comes to him in *Iliad* 24; of the

(Ismarus, Lotus, *Cyclops*; Aeolus, Laestrygonians, *Circe*; Sirens, Scylla
and Charybdis, *Cattle of the Sun*). And the return of Odysseus to
Circe's island after the Visit to the Underworld is difficult to understand as part of an originally intended pattern of events, but easy to
understand as consequence of the insertion of the Visit as an afterthought into a pattern that did not originally include it. (For if Circe
is to give Odysseus—as she does—parting advice about his impending
encounters with the Sirens, Scylla, etc., the insertion of an extra and
important adventure cannot without great complications be made
after the parting advice and before the adventures to which the advice
refers: it is simpler therefore to break the Circe episode near its end,
sending Odysseus from her to the Underworld and bringing him back
again to receive her parting advice about the perils that lie next ahead.)
The fact that the insertion modifies an original design does not of
course compel the inference that it was made by someone other than
the original designer.

It is a curious circumstance that in *both* of the Homeric poems there
is one book that appears to have been inserted as an afterthought
into a construction that did not originally include it. For such seems
to be the case with Book 10 of the *Iliad* as well as with Book 11 of
the *Odyssey*. Book 10 of the *Iliad* tells the story of the adventure of
Diomede and Odysseus in the night after the first defeat of the Greeks;
in it they kill the Trojan Dolon and a number of Thracians and carry
off the horses of Rhesus the Thracian king. An ancient commentator
recorded that this was held by some in his day to have been originally
a poem by Homer separate from the *Iliad*, and first included in the
Iliad 'by Peisistratus'—i.e. at the time in the sixth century when regular
recitations of the *Iliad* and *Odyssey* appear to have been instituted
as a feature of the Great Panathenaic Festival. The ancient commentator's report is not in itself conclusive evidence; nor is the undoubted
fact that Book 10 could be excised from the *Iliad* without leaving any
trace that it ever was in it, the remarkable events it relates being never
afterwards mentioned; nor is the equally undoubted fact that the in-
clusion of Book 10 makes the night it refers to most improbably
crowded with events—for before setting out on their expedition
Diomede and Odysseus have already since sundown (8. 485) attended
an assembly of the army (9.9 ff.) and a council of the chiefs (9.89 ff.),
and Odysseus has gone on the unsuccessful mission of entreaty to
Achilles (9. 169 ff.). But taken together these considerations do suggest
that this book was not part of the original design; and there is reason

to believe that it was composed at a different time, since it contains a considerable number of lines and phrases which are common to it and to the *Odyssey* but to no other book of the *Iliad*: for this see lines 214, 243, 292-4, 284, 457, 530, 534, 540, 556, 576. This reinforces the probability that the book is a later insertion into the *Iliad*, but does not necessarily carry the implication that it was made (or inserted) by someone other than the maker of the *Iliad* itself.

Unlike Book 11 of the *Odyssey*, which makes a valuable contribution to the overall effect of the poem, Book 10 of the *Iliad* makes no such contribution, though it is a good story in itself.

28. Incongruities felt by some to be of crucial significance have by others been felt to be trivial or non-existent. Many examples might be offered, but two will suffice to make plain what is meant.

In the ninth book of the *Iliad* Agamemnon sends honourable envoys to Achilles with the offer of the return of Briseïs and copious gifts to induce him to relent and come to the aid of the Greeks. The comments of Achilles' friends Phoenix and Ajax make it plain that such a price should satisfy the honour of any reasonable man. But Achilles rejects it outright. His bitter resentment of Agamemnon's insult is in no way appeased; and he scorns Agamemnon's gifts. And he declares that he will not return to the battlefield until the Trojan advance threatens his own encampment.

In the sixteenth book, when the Greeks are in a desperate situation (but Achilles' encampment is not yet threatened), Patroclus reproaches Achilles with his hardness of heart and asks to be allowed to go to the rescue himself, if Achilles will not. Achilles relents to that extent and agrees. But he is still bitterly resentful when he thinks of the way Agamemnon has insulted him. As he sees the Trojans pressing on he says: 'Soon would they have filled (or, fill) the gullies with their dead if the lord Agamemnon had (or, had had) respect for me'. And a little later he warns Patroclus to turn back once he has driven the enemy from the ships, and not press his success further, 'so that you may win great honour for me, and the Greeks may give me back the fair young girl and add rich gifts besides'.

How, it is asked by some, can Achilles speak in such terms when only a few hours earlier Agamemnon has offered him handsome compensation? And how can he be concerned to get gifts now, when he has only lately said he had no wish for those which Agamemnon offered?

Some readers think that all this is fully in accordance with what

we have seen of Achilles' character and state of mind. In Boo[k] is governed by passion and behaving in a quite irrational way. I[n] 16 he is cooling somewhat but is still irrational. The insult do[ne] by Agamemnon still rankles bitterly, unappeased now, as it wa[s] by the offer made him in the earlier scene. But he is softening t[o] the Greeks who are suffering from his punishment of Agam[emnon]. As for the interest he now shows in the getting of gifts, that, [sign] of his beginning to relent, follows naturally on the warning [he had] from Phoenix in Book 9. Phoenix there reminded him how M[eleager] first refused to help his fellow-citizens when they offered h[im] rewards, and then yielded to his wife's entreaties and gave h[elp] unconditionally, with the result that he got no gifts at all. And [Ajax] pointed out that this brought loss of honour.

Other readers feel an irreconcilable contradiction between A[chilles'] words in Book 9 and his later words in Book 16: Achilles th[ey say] may be irrational, but not as irrational as that. Hence they in[fer that] Book 9 has been inserted as an improvement or afterthought [on an] earlier version of the story in which no offer of amends wa[s made] and that this alteration was made either (a) by the same po[et who] made the first version or (b) by another.

There is no dogma to be revered in this matter. Every reade[r makes] up his own mind for himself.

29. In the first book of the *Odyssey* the goddess Athena, wis[hing to] prepare the drastic vengeance which is to overtake the wo[oers of] Penelope later in the story, and meanwhile to rouse Telema[chus to] assert himself against them and to undertake the journey to P[elopon]nese which the design of the poem requires, comes to Ithaca d[isguised] as a merchant captain and pretending to be an old acquaintanc[e of the] absent Odysseus. Telemachus tells his visitor about the suit[ors'] insolence and what he supposes to be his mother's indecision, [and re]ceives in return several pieces of advice.

First, he is to give the suitors formal and public notice to [quit the] house; if Penelope herself wishes to remarry she can go back [to her] father's house and let her own kinsfolk make the necessary a[rrange]ments.

Secondly, Telemachus is to go to the mainland and find out v[hether] other Greek princes who have come back from Troy can gi[ve him] definite news of his father, alive or dead.

Thirdly, his further action is to depend on what he lear[ns from] this inquiry. If he hears that his father is still somewhere aliv[e and]

courtyard of Odysseus' house at the beginning of the *Odyssey*; of Calypso's grotto and garden, the Cyclops' cave, Phorcys' haven where Odysseus is landed by the Phaeacians, Eumaeus' hut and yard, and so on. Or again the description may be of an elaborate process—the arming of a hero for combat is an obvious example, but there are other notable instances, such as the harnessing of Priam's waggon before his bold venture in *Iliad* 24, and the building of Odysseus' raft before he sets out on his eventful homeward voyage. Sometimes a particular object is elaborately dwelt on—Agamemnon's sceptre at the opening of the assembly in *Iliad* 2, Pandarus' bow as he prepares for his treacherous and fateful shot in *Iliad* 4, Nestor's cup in the scene before the crucial appearance of Patroclus in *Iliad* 11, the cup from which Achilles pours libation as he sends Patroclus out to battle in *Iliad* 16. The effect is to stimulate the visual imagination in readiness for what is next to follow in the story.

31. Scenes that contain an element strongly evocative of a specific feeling or sensation, promoting an effect of felt as well as seen reality, are often placed at a turning point of the story, where one phase ends and another is about to begin: as when Telemachus lies snug under his sheepskin thinking of tomorrow's enterprise, at the end of *Odyssey* 1; or when Odysseus is welcomed by the old dog as he stands disguised at his own house door in *Odyssey* 17; or when the Trojans camp on the plain at the end of *Iliad* 8, exhilarated by their late success and looking forward to renewal of the battle next day; or when Ajax's spear-head is cut off in *Iliad* 16, ending his long resistance and letting the fire be lit that is signal for the turning of the Trojans' victory to defeat. In all these passages, and others like them, elements are combined which express both an end and a beginning in the development of the story, together with an element that animates the scene by stirring a sharp response of recognition in the hearer or reader.

32. The variety of the smiles is instructive; so it is worth while to specify further. Thus, Hera smiles when Hephaestus consoles her embarrassment (*Iliad* 1.595): a grateful smile. Agamemnon smiles as he withdraws the words that have offended Odysseus (4.356): a conciliatory smile. Zeus smiles as he tells the tearful Aphrodite that she has herself to thank for her rough handling by Diomede (5.426): a smile of gentle and amused reproof. Hector smiles at the sight of his baby son (6.403): a smile of fond and fatherly pleasure. Ajax has a smile on his grim countenance as he strides forward to do battle (7.

212): a menacing and confident smile. Odysseus smiles at Dolon's confession that he hoped to win the horses of Achilles as reward (10.400): a smile of amused superiority. Hera smiles as she receives from Aphrodite the magic brassière (?) that she has obtained by false pretence (14.222): a smile ambiguous between gratitude and private satisfaction. Zeus smiles when he has made Hera submit to his will (15.47): a smile of satisfied superiority. Hera smiles as she slaps Artemis' face and makes her cry (21.491): the cruel smile of the triumphant bully. Calypso smiles at Odysseus' cautious reaction to her promise to send him on his way (*Odyssey* 5.180): the smile of tolerant affection towards a familiar idiosyncrasy of the loved one. Menelaus smiles at Telemachus' tactful handling of the offer of an unsuitable present (4.609): an approving smile. Telemachus smiles at his now-recognized father behind the back of the unconscious Eumaeus (14. 476): the conspiratorial smile of pleasure in a shared secret. Odysseus smiles at the frightened herald as he spares his life (22.371): the smile of amused superiority.

In all these passages the word used is the word for 'smile' proper (*meidáō*). In others there is the word for 'laughter' (*gelōs*) and its related verb, which may include laughing features even without sound. Andromache, who has been crying, laughs with her husband at their baby's fear of Hector's helmet (*Iliad* 6.471); and a little later as she takes the child in her arms the end of the laugh is still on her tearful face (484). Hera, smarting from Zeus' rough rebuke (15.102), responds to the greeting of the other gods with a laugh 'of the lips but not the eyes', i.e. a forced and mirthless laugh or smile. Penelope, inspired by Athene with an irrational impulse to display herself before the suitors (*Odyssey* 18.163) laughs in a vague and embarrassed way as she tells her attendant of the whim which is puzzling to herself. The suitors laugh in anticipation of sport to come as they crowd around the quarrelling beggars (18.40), and lift their arms and 'die for laughing' when Irus is knocked out (100). The maids look at one another and laugh (i.e. giggle) when the stranger offers to relieve them of their job of keeping the braziers burning in the hall (18.320). In the uncanny atmosphere that develops as the crisis approaches the suitors laugh hysterically as if possessed (20.347). Telemachus cannot control a (nervous) urge to laugh (21.105) when his mother tells the suitors that their chance is now to come. The old nurse runs upstairs to bring the good news to her mistress laughing exultantly (*kanchaloōn*, a different word this time), as she falls over her feet with excitement in her haste (23.1).

One purpose of this long review is to show how extensive and accurate and particular is the poet's awareness of traits of human demeanour that we can still recognize, as true to life no less today than then. Another purpose is to show that there are two different ways in which this awareness is communicated to those to whom he speaks. For sometimes, in the case of the 'laughs' especially, the quality and the significance of the laugh are made recognizable by quite specific indications; while at other times, in the case of the 'smiles' especially, the quality and significance of the smile is left to be inferred from the context—because the poet can rely on the experience of human behaviour that his audience shares with him to perform the act of recognition. His method is economical: to the extent that it can count on assistance of his audience's imagination it is content to do so; where more is required, it provides it.

The same difference of procedure can be observed in respect of sound-words. Many of these are very precisely expressive, and confined in their applications accordingly: bleating and whimpering and chattering and thudding and so on. But the verb *iachō* (which represents always some striking kind of sound) is used in a surprising variety of applications: for instance, of the roar of a blazing fire (*Iliad* 23.216); the hiss of hot metal plunged into cold water (*Odyssey* 9.392); the twang of a bowstring (*Iliad* 4.125); the blast of a trumpet (*Iliad* 18.219); the war-cry of a warrior (*Iliad* 19.424); and the wail of a frightened baby (*Iliad* 6.468). The sounds are all very different one from another. Yet the word used throughout is the same. The imagination supplies from experience the distinctive sound appropriate in each case.

33. *Nestor's* reminiscences: *Iliad* 1.260 ff., 7.123 ff., 11.670 ff., 23.626 ff. His tact in awkward situations: 1.260 ff. (quarrel of chiefs), 7.123 ff. (hesitation of Greeks at Hector's challenge), 9.52 ff. and 95 ff. (Diomede's bluntness and Agamemnon's embarrassment). His adroitness in taking opportunity: 9.52 ff. and 95 ff. (to get Agamemnon to try to appease Achilles), 11.795 ff. (to get Patroclus to appeal to Achilles). Note also expertise due to experience: 2.360 ff. (organization of army), 4.293 ff. (disposition of his own force), 23.306 ff. (hints on chariot-driving).

34. *Odysseus* as man for a mission: 1.311 ff. (return of Chryseis to her father), 3.205 (Embassy to Troy before the war), 9.192 ff. (the deputation to Achilles), 11.767 (recruiting for the expedition). Prompt and decided action: 2.182 ff. (checking the stampede of the assembly,

a strongly significant scene). Cool judgement: 2.182 ff. (as above), 14.82 ff. (checking Agamemnon's panic), 19.155 ff. (checking Achilles' impatience). Persuasive speaker: 3.216 ff. (Antenor's testimony), 9.225 ff. (carefully calculated appeal to Achilles). Courage as act of will: 11.401 ff. (a significant soliloquy, with which may be compared—not to their disadvantage—the soliloquies of Menelaus at 17.90 ff., and Agenor at 21.552 ff. and Hector at 22.98 ff.).

35. *Menelaus'* relative inferiority in strength and skill: 7.104 ff. (held back by the others from accepting Hector's challenge and told by Agamemnon not to be a fool—a strongly significant scene). His sensible acceptance of his own limitations, without neglect of duty: 17.91 ff. (a strongly significant soliloquy). His willingness and perseverance in face of danger: 3.21 ff. (gladly accepts Paris' challenge), 7.94 ff. (is ready to accept Hector's challenge), 4.150 ff. and 183 ff. (keeps calm when wounded), 11.465 ff. (helps to rescue Odysseus), 13.581–642 (active in the battle), 17 (kills Euphorbus in revenge for Patroclus, fights in defence of Patroclus' body and finally helps to carry it back to Achilles). Recognizes his obligation to those who suffer for his sake: 3.98 ff. (speech as he accepts Paris' challenge), 17.92 (soliloquy, as he stands over Patroclus' body).

36. *Agamemnon's* imposing presence: 2.477 (described by the poet at the marshalling of the army), 3.169 (admired by Priam), 2.100 ff. (the emphasis on his sceptre and its significance), 11.15 ff. (the splendour of his accoutrements), 11.91–266 (his impressive though temporary achievements in combat). His ineffectiveness in a crisis: 2.162 ff. (a strongly significant scene, in which Odysseus seizes the sceptre from him and assumes command), 9.38 ff. (despair after first defeat), 14.65 ff. (panic as things get worse). His overbearing way with inferiors: 1.24 ff. (his rebuff of Chryses, a strongly significant scene). His avarice: 1.122 (Achilles' gibe), 3.288 ff. (concern for 'damages').

(Other words and acts of Agamemnon may be variously understood. He appears more concerned for himself than for Menelaus after the latter's wounding (4.169 ff.). After his apparently handsome offer of amends to Achilles, he concludes 'and let him submit himself to me, who am his overlord' (9.160). When wounded he retires from the field (unlike Diomede in 5 and Glaucus in 12) without reference to his functions as commander (11.267). When offered reconciliation by Achilles he appears (19.81) to rebuke the applause of the army, and in admitting his own error he lays the whole blame on supernatural influence, and puts himself on a par with the king of the gods (9.90–136), whose victim however he claims to be.)

37. *Diomede* accepts rebuke from Agamemnon on the field, and administers rebuke to him in return at the assembly (4.411 ff. and 9.31 ff.), in accordance with his understanding of the rules of conduct. In debate he regularly waits until there is a silence, speaks incisively, and wins immediate assent (7.938 ff., 9.29 ff., 9.695 ff., 14.109 ff.). His blunt words to Agamemnon in 9 are requital for Agamemnon's to him in 4, and give Nestor the opportunity to move Agamemnon to offer amends to Achilles: his character thus becomes part of the mechanism that develops the story. His furious activity in 5 can be seen as reaction to Agamemnon's rebuke in 4, though this is nowhere said to be the case.

38. *Ajax* is tallest and biggest of the Greek chieftains (as seen by Priam 3.227). He has a long stride, and a grim smile on his face under heavy brows as he marches forward for his duel with Hector (7.212 ff.). He carries a big shield of seven layers of hide (7.220): it is 'like a tower' (7.219, 11.485, 17.128). The Greeks hope the lot will choose him to be their champion against Hector (7.179, 182): and indeed he twice strikes Hector to the ground (7.271, 14.418). He is called to the aid of Odysseus (11.464), and of Menestheus (12.343), and the defence of Patroclus' body (17.119). He protects the retreat of his comrades in the rout (11.570 etc.), and the wall (12.318 ff.), and the ships (15.674 ff. etc.), and Patroclus' body (17 *passim*), and the bearers who finally carry it off the field (17.716 ff.). In the deputation to Achilles he speaks last, and briefly, appealing to reason and friendship (9.630 ff.).

39. *Hera's* spite 4.31 ff.; she is suspicious of Zeus 1.536 ff.; resentful 4.25 ff.; deceiving 14.153 ff.; afraid 1.568, 15.34 ff. *Athena* suppressing her resentment 4.22, 8.459 (contrast as exception 8.357 ff.); acting with Zeus' permission 4.69 ff., 22.185 ff.—in both cases to win her purpose by unscrupulous deceit; repressing Achilles' angry impulse 1.206 ff.; friend to Diomede 5.1 ff., 23.388 ff., to Diomede and Odysseus 10.274 ff., to Odysseus 2.166 ff., 11.437 ff., 23.768 ff.; overruling Ares 15.121 ff., beating him in battle 5.855 ff., 21.391 ff. *Hephaestus* as cripple and artisan 18.368 ff. (and in 1.571 ff. it is no doubt his cripple's awkwardness that moves the gods to mirth). *Thetis* sorrowful 1.413 ff. and 505, 18.52 ff., 94 ff., 428 ff., 24.84 f., 131 f. *Zeus'*

predominance, and rude methods with his subject gods 1.533 ff., 565 ff., 589 ff., 8.5 ff., 15.13 ff., 104 ff., 127 ff., 173 ff.; his nagging wife 1.518 ff. etc.; his grief for his son 16.433 ff.; his regrets for Troy 4.44 ff., for Hector 22.168 ff; pity for human suffering 17.201 ff., 445 ff.

40. *Zeus* genially presiding *Odyssey* 1.26–79, 5.3–42; tactfully pacifying 13.125–58 (and cf. 24.472–86). *Athena's* political adroitness 1.19–62; her appreciation of Odysseus as a kindred spirit 13.221–332.

41a. In the *Odyssey* Antinoüs takes the lead in proposing the murder of Telemachus (*Odyssey* 4.669), and the fight between the rival beggars (18.34 ff.), and the order of attempts upon the bow (21.140). He is first to insult the disguised Odysseus (17.445 ff.), and is first to be killed (22.8 ff.).

41b. *Eurymachus* takes the lead only to ingratiate himself with Penelope (16.434 promising protection to Telemachus—with duplicity, 448; complimenting Penelope herself 18.244). He has won over the servants Melanthius (17.257) and Melantho (18.325). His suit is favoured by Penelope's family (15.16) and he is courted by the Ithacans (15.518). He speaks as a bully at the Ithacan assembly (2.178 ff.), and with a sneer to the disguised Odysseus (18.349 ff.). He tries in vain to lay the blame for the suitors' misdeeds on Antinoüs (22.44 ff.).

42. *Eurycleia* is seen lighting Telemachus to bed and putting away his clothes (1.428 ff.); presiding over the household stores (2.345 ff.); arranging the furniture in the hall (17.32); directing the household duties of the maids (20.147 ff.). Her emotional reactions are often reported, 2.362 (to Telemachus' proposed adventure), 17.33 (to his arrival home), 19.361 (to the thought of her absent master), 19.471 ff. (to her recognition of him), 22.407 (to the sight of the suitors slain), 23.1 ff. (to the excitement of bringing the news to Penelope). She is usually addressed as *maia* by the family, and she usually says 'dear child' without discrimination in speaking to any of them. A pleasant touch is her anxiety to bring Odysseus decent clothes before all else, when they meet after his suitor-slaying (22.487).

43. *Eumaeus* is observed at leisure in 14, 15.301–492, 16.1–155 with

452–81, and 17.1–395 with 507–606; and enumeration of particulars here would be confusing rather than helpful. Worth noting in addition to the facts mentioned in the text are the especially expressive scene at the end of 14, when he goes out in ugly weather to be near his beasts through the night; and his addiction to sentiments typical of his condition—14.67 ff. (what a faithful servant can hope for from a kind master), 15.374 ff. (the need for a talk from time to time with the mistress, and little marks of appreciation), 17.319 ff. (disapproval of those who neglect their duties). He is habitually addressed by Telemachus as *atta*, and addresses him as 'my child' or 'dear child'.

44. *Telemachus'* relations with his mother: 1.353 (sudden assumption of authority, which she, surprised, accepts), 2.373 ff. (concealing his departure from her), 17.46 (abruptness to her on his return), 21.350 ff. (he orders her from the hall); 15.15–23 (Athena suggests to him—i.e. he is ready to believe—that she may be about to marry Eurymachus: cf. also 16.33 ff.); 18.215–29 (a temporary reassertion of maternal authority); 19.159 and 532 (Penelope feels that he would be glad to see her go, so as to stop the wasting of his property). The servants and Telemachus: 1.428 ff. (Eurycleia's solicitous attentions); 2.363 ff. (her wail of protest on hearing of his plan); 16.14 ff. (Eumaeus' emotional welcome on his return); 17.30 ff. (the maids' emotional welcome on his return). His father's friends: 3.123 ff. (Nestor thinks him just like his father); 4.140 ff. (Helen and Menelaus think the same). First encounters with the fugitive Theoclymenus and with the pretended castaway: 15.271–81 (he accepts the role of protector to Theoclymenus), 16.42–45 (the supposed castaway's deference and the young man's condescension).

45. *Hector.* The moment of almost final success: *Iliad* 16.114 ff. (fire in the ships). Fatal over-confidence: 18.249 ff. (Polydamas' advice rejected). Remorse: 22.99 ff. (his thoughts as he stands alone outside the city-wall). The gods' regard for him: 24.22 ff. and 66 ff. (indignation in heaven and Zeus' concern). Honour from his people: 24.724-end (lamentation in Troy, and the funeral). The irony of his temporary success: 1.503 ff. (Thetis' prayer and Zeus' promise), 8.473 ff. and 15.54 ff. (Zeus expounds the whole design). Moments of failure: 7.263 ff. (Ajax strikes him down), 11.349 ff. (Diomede strikes him down), 14.402 ff. (Ajax strikes him down). Domestic scene: 6.392–502 (meeting with wife and child).

46. *Odysseus.* A well-loved king: *Odyssey* 2.233 ff. (Mentor's speech in the Ithacan assembly). A well-loved master: 14.40 ff., 137 ff., 169 ff. (Eumaeus' testimony). Remarkable feats of strength: 8.186 (the casual quoit-cast), 18.90 ff. (the 'light blow' and its devastating effect), 21.404 ff. (the easy stringing of the bow that none could bend). The man longing and longed for: 5.210 (*tēs aien eëldeai*) and 23.54 (*nun d' ēdē tode makron eëldōr ektetelestai*).

47. *Patroclus'* kindness is often mentioned. Thus Zeus speaks of Achilles' 'brave and gentle comrade' (*Iliad* 17.204). Menelaus in the fighting over his body calls on the other Greeks to remember his 'gentleness' and how 'it was his way to be kind to all' (17.669 ff.). Briseis mourns for him as one who was 'always kind' (19.300). The other chiefs weep for 'their gentle comrade' as his bones are gathered from the pyre after his burning. No other of the Greek heroes is spoken of like this. On the other side, Hector's kindness and gentleness is remembered by Helen in her lament over his body (24.762 ff.).

48. We do not know with any accuracy how Homeric poetry was pronounced by its first performers. But this (perhaps surprisingly) does not much matter. People for centuries have been charmed by the sounds and rhythms of ancient Greek poetry pronounced according to their own very diverse local styles. And so with Latin poetry too. The Victorians read Virgil in a pronunciation barely intelligible to the present generation; but they certainly did not take less delight than we do in the music of Virgil's verse. The fact of the matter seems to be that the difference between long and short, broad and thin, smooth and rough, awkwardness and elegance of collocation, abides with little change in all systems; and so naturally do the patterns formed by the repetition of sounds similar to one another. The quality of individual vowel sounds (especially) may indeed vary very much from time to time and from place to place. But what we like or dislike in this respect depends very much on what we are used to. So that we can seldom wrong a poet by sounding his vowels in a way familiar and congenial to ourselves—though we may greatly grieve others who are accustomed to sound them differently, especially if they are compatriots of the poet and we are not.

The following suggestions for the pronunciation of Greek words transliterated into the English alphabet in this book are (like the transliterations themselves) conventional, and by no means scientific. For an interesting scientific enquiry into the pronunciation of ancient

Greek—with reference primarily to the classical period—see W. S. Allen, *Vox Graeca* (Cambridge, second edition, 1974).

1. Consonants as in English, except that *ch* should be as in Scottish *loch*. But doubled consonants should be sounded twice as in Italian: *ellabe* is *el-labe*, *ennepe* is *en-nepe*, etc.

2. Vowels as follows: *a* as in *at*; *ā* as in *ah*; *e* as in *bet*; *ē* as in *whey* (not as in *bee*); *i* as in *in*; *ī* as in *marine* (not as in *die*); *o* as in *on*; *ō* as in *oh*; *u* as in *put*; *u* as in *cue* (or *boo*). Consecutive vowels (except in diphthongs, on which see below) are sounded separately: e.g. *eēldōr*, or *aēdōn* are trisyllables, *boös* a disyllable. When occasionally a pair of vowels (other than a diphthong) are to be treated as one syllable the fact is indicated thus: *theômen, hūmêas*.

3. Diphthongs are *ai*, as in *aisle*; *au* as in *out* (not as in *taut*); *ei* as in *whey* (cf. *ē*): *eu* or *ēu* as in *neuter*; *oi* as in *quoit*; *ou* as in *dour* (not as in *sour*). When the vowels in any of these pairs are not to make a diphthong but are to be sounded separately, the fact is indicated thus: *eü, oïs, nēlei, aütmē*.

4. By convention most English readers of ancient Greek read it with the same stress accent as they do their own language, with some concession to the beat of the verse.

49. One can quite often identify the equivalents in tone of such English expressions as: 'We haven't often seen you here lately' (*Iliad* 18.386); 'I mustn't sit down . . .' (*Iliad* 11.648); 'I'll soon teach you who to take orders from' (*Odyssey* 21.369); 'There's nothing for it but . . .' (*Iliad* 5.218); 'What you say is quite right, but . . .' (*Odyssey* 22.486, etc.); 'Let's think what's the best way to manage this . . .' (*Odyssey* 17.274); and so on.

50. *pappa* is the word with which Nausicaa addresses her father, and no one will doubt what is its English equivalent. Other modes of address current in the poems strike an equally familiar note. Thus, old Eurycleia, who has nursed Odysseus and Telemachus as babies, still says *philon tekos* ('dear child') or *teknon emon* ('my child') to both of them, and to her mistress Penelope as well: she also still calls Penelope *numpha philē* ('dear bride' = 'dear young mistress'), as she used to do when Penelope came as a bride to the house twenty years before. All the family for their part call her *maia* (= ? 'nanna', or 'mother' in one of its colloquial uses). Old Eumaeus says *philon tekos* to Telemachus (but *basileia* = 'my lady' to Penelope); and Telemachus in return calls him *atta* (= ? 'uncle' in a colloquial use still current in

recent times). Old Phoenix in the *Iliad* is addressed as *atta* by Achilles, whom he has adored since infancy; it is not surprising if others have picked up the habit (as Menelaus at *Iliad* 17.561 appears to have done).

In a range of contexts wider than that of the family *pepon* (= ? 'comrade') is used between peers, usually by the elder of two or the one who is taking the lead—by Zeus to Poseidon, Agamemnon to Menelaus, Sarpedon to Glaucus, and reciprocally by Menelaus and Ajax in the fighting over Patroclus' body (one being superior in status and the other in efficiency). When the Cyclops in the *Odyssey* calls his ram *pepon* it reveals a special and pathetic relationship between the lonely giant and his beast. *ētheie* is a mode of address that marks respect mingled with affection: it is used by Eumaeus towards his revered master Odysseus, and by Hector's brothers towards Hector— by the apologetic Paris at *Iliad* 6.518 and by Athena pretending to be Deiphobus at 22.229 and 239 (where it appears that Deiphobus is best loved and most devoted of all the brothers). Lastly, *tetta* is said by Diomede to Sthenelus in the sharp rebuke that he administers to him at *Iliad* 4.412. Presumably it corresponds to the English 'Sir!' when sternly spoken, or to 'Sirra' in an older style.

The vocative *daimonie* ($-\bar{e}$, *-oi*) at the beginning of a speech lends a tone of remonstrance to what follows, but a tone that may vary very widely in quality according to context—it may be (and frequently is) angry, resentful, scornful, impatient, stern, etc.: but it may also be anxiously entreating (as in Andromache's appeal to Hector at *Iliad* 6.407), or affectionate (as in his reply at 486), or good-natured (as when Eumaeus cuts short Odysseus' expressions of gratitude at *Odyssey* 14.443), or ironical (as when a warrior taunts an adversary with holding back at *Iliad* 13.448 and 810), or cautionary (as when Antinous checks his companions' indiscretion at *Odyssey* 4.774), or mild but firm (as when Odysseus resists Irus' attempt to oust him at *Odyssey* 18.15). When Odysseus' crew so address him in proposing a move from Circe's island (*Odyssey* 10.472) they are perhaps reproaching him for too long delay. When Priam so addresses Hecuba in telling her of Iris' bidding that he go and appeal to Achilles, and his wish to comply with it, he is perhaps anticipating the loud objection that in fact follows and is overruled by him (*Iliad* 24.194). In the scene towards the end of the *Odyssey* (23.166–180) in which Odysseus appears to be becoming impatient at Penelope's hesitation he addresses her as *daimoniē* and she him as *daimonie* in her reply: the tone of this exchange may be imagined differently by different readers, and it will be seen from what has been said above that the usage of the word allows various possibilities.

51. The copiousness of the Homeric vocabulary (and specifically *of the non-repetitive element* in it) can be illustrated further by reference (as example only) to a set of adverbs whose distinctive form makes them a conveniently identifiable sample. Such are *agelēdon* = in a herd; *apostadon* = standing at a distance; *botrūdon* = in clusters; *embadon* = on foot; *exanaphandon* = openly; *īladon* = in crowds; *klangēdon* = with loud cries; *panthūmadon* = passionately; *sphairēdon* = as one throws a ball; *phalangēdon* = in solid ranks; *amblēdēn* = lifting up the voice; *amboladen* = bubbling; *emplegden* = impulsively; *epigrabdēn* = with a grazing stroke; *epiligdēn* = with a grazing or glancing stroke; *metadromadēn* = running after; *homartēdēn* = all together; *parablēdēn* = provocatively; *protropadēn* = in headlong flight; *tmēdēn* = with a cutting stroke; *hupoblēdēn* = interrupting; *amogētī* = without effort; *anidrōtī* = without sweat; *autonuchī* = this very night. These adverbs occur each once only in the 28,000 lines that the two poems between them comprise.

52. The epithets attached to persons' names no doubt originated in a habit current once in real life, of distinguishing some individuals by patronymic or descriptive surnames. Peleus' son Achilles and fair-haired Menelaus and far-ruling Agamemnon have their counterparts, as do others like them in the prose sagas of the Norsemen: Gunnar Lambi's son, Erik the Red, Gudmund the Powerful, and so on. However, the Homeric tradition usually excludes uncomplimentary and unpoetical designations: no one in *Iliad* or *Odyssey* is named like Eyvind Braggart or Thorhalla Chatterbox or Thorkill Foulmouth, or for that matter, Ketil Flatnose.

53. Conspicuous also, though less conspicuous than the repetition of lines and phrases, is the repetition of motifs. A story-teller's imagination has a natural tendency to repeat itself, especially when the stories have to be developed impromptu. Audiences for their part are found to form an affection for some familiar themes. And variations on such themes are a form of novelty in which both teller and hearers take pleasure. The Quarrel of Heroes which begins the *Iliad* has an evident kinship with the Quarrel of Heroes which Demodocus takes for his first subject in his singing for Alcinous' guests (*Odyssey* 8). The Arming of a Hero repeats itself in the *Iliad* in the arming of Paris (3.328 ff.), of Diomede and Odysseus (10.254 ff.),

of Agamemnon (11.17 ff.), of Patroclus (16.130 ff.), and of Achilles (19.367 ff.). The Catalogues of Greeks and Trojans (*Iliad* 2) have a miniature counterpart in the Catalogue of the Myrmidons (16.168 ff.). Glaucus recites his Genealogy to Diomede (6.150 ff.), and Aeneas recites his to Achilles (20.208 ff.). These are examples only.

Repetitions abound in the *Odyssey* also, and not only in the recognitions and near recognitions, and peltings and deceptive tales that are frequent in the Ithacan scenes in the second half of the poem. Menelaus and Helen (in Book 4) remember Odysseus in past situations which situations in the present story are going to resemble: disguised in rags as a beggar, impressive as he stood stripped for a bout of wrestling, checking a comrade's impulse to cry out when safety called for silence. Menelaus himself has had experiences similar to some which Odysseus has had or is about to have: he has been held starving on an island by adverse winds, he has been helped by a friendly sea-nymph (Eidothea), he has been referred for advice and information to a wizard seer (Proteus). The adventures of Odysseus when we come to them prove to duplicate one another in certain respects: there are the would-be detainers Calypso and Circe in their island dwellings, the giant cannibal Cyclops and the giant cannibal Laestrygonians, the narcotic singing of the Sirens and the narcotic fruit of the Lotus, the carefree Phaeacians who help the hero home and the carefree Aeolus who would have done so but for the crew's inquisitiveness, the shipwreck brought about by angry Poseidon and the shipwreck brought about by the angry Sun-god. It is hard to say whether these duplications are due to our poet's invention and its way of working, or to an inheritance received by him of variants developed long before.

Repetition of motif often serves a calculated purpose, for instance: a contrast pointed by a symmetry (the duels of *Iliad* 3 and 22); a climax achieved through a series (the insults offered successively to Odysseus by Antinous, Eurymachus and Ctesippus); the intellectual pleasure to be drawn from variation on a theme (recognition of Odysseus by the dog, through the scar, and through the shared secret); the indication of a trait of character (Nestor's reminiscences in *Iliad* 1, 7, 11, etc.). Indeed, in the *Iliad* repetitions of motif are basic to its simple but effective overall design: the Anger of Achilles against Agamemnon succeeded by his intenser Anger against Hector, the defeat of the Greeks in the second battle succeeded by their still more disastrous defeat in the third.

54. Achilles is pouring libations on the pyre. The metrical foot called

spondee (− −), which is repeated six times in this line, gets its name from the Greek word for libation, because it was used in formulae accompanying that act.

55. P. Mazon in *Introduction à l'Iliade* (Paris 1942), pp. 298-9. G.M. Sargeaunt in *Classical Studies* (London, Chatto and Windus, 1929), pp. 1-16 (on the Odyssey).

Appendix 1

Supposed or real schemes of construction in the *Iliad* and *Odyssey*

The content of the *Iliad* can be divided into sections as follows:

Books 1–2, the Wrath of Achilles explodes and he withdraws his services; 3–7, battle begins between the Greeks and the Trojans and at first is inconclusive; 8–9, the Greeks are beaten and appeal to Achilles, who is unrelenting; (10, a detachable interlude, the Doloneia); 11–15, the Greek camp is stormed and their ships are threatened; 16–17, Patroclus goes to the rescue and is killed by Hector; 18–22, the direction of the Wrath is changed, and Achilles returns to the field and kills Hector; 23–4, Patroclus and Hector are buried, and the Wrath is at last worked out.

From this division emerges (or seems to emerge) a pattern of units in the form 2 + 5 + 2 + 5 (or 6) + 2 + 5 + 2. For though the division of the poem into 'books' can hardly be due to its composer, the 'books' do correspond to phases in the development of its story, and so perhaps to units of composition.

Critics vary in their assessment of this apparent pattern. To some it is impressive, and indicative of an intention on the part of the composer. To others it is illusory, the divisions assumed being in their view arbitrary. It has certainly been found helpful by some readers as an aid to memory.

The content of the *Odyssey* divides easily into groups of four books apiece, thus:

Books 1–4, the state of affairs in Ithaca and Telemachus' journey to Peloponnese in quest for news of his father; 5–8, Odysseus' departure from Calypso, shipwreck and reception by the Phaeacians; 9–12, Odysseus tells his hosts the story of his past adventures; 13–16, Odysseus' arrival in Ithaca and sojourn in Eumaeus' hut; 17–20, Odysseus' arrival in his own house, and events there precedent to the crisis; 21–4, crisis, dénouement and conclusion.

The four-book units thus delineated form also a series of units of ascending magnitude, as follows: 1–4 (four books), Ithaca and Telemachus; 5–12 (eight books), Odysseus' adventures on his way home from Troy; 13–24 (twelve books), Odysseus' arrival home and vengeance on his enemies and reunion with his wife and family.

Appendix 2

The topography of the *Iliad* and *Odyssey*

In the *Iliad* the Greeks are encamped, and their ships drawn up, on the south shore of the Hellespont (15.233, etc.). Opposite is the Thracian mainland, and out in the Aegean are the islands of Imbros and Tenedos (13.33 etc.). The town of Troy, strongly walled, stands inland on a modest eminence (since men 'go up' to it, and it has a citadel), at no great distance from the Greek camp. Mount Ida is in the background. A gate of the town called the Scaean Gate apparently looks towards the Greek camp; not far from it is an oak-tree, noted as a landmark (6.237, 9.354, 11.170); somewhere also in the vicinity of the town is a wild fig-tree (6.433, 22.145; less obviously 11.167), and two springs (one cold and the other hot) with stone troughs near at hand which the women of Troy in peace-time used for washing clothes—it is by these that Hector runs (22.147 ff.) in his flight from Achilles before the duel in which he meets his death.

The battles (except when the Greek camp itself is penetrated for a time) are fought in the plain between camp and town, bounded on either side (6.4) by two streams, Simoeis and Xanthus (also called Scamander): in one passage the courses of these are said (5.774) to join (which would make a nonsense), or perhaps rather to converge. The victorious Trojans at the end of the second day's fighting bivouac on the plain 'between the ships and the stream of Xanthus'. A ford over the Xanthus is mentioned several times, but never crossed by anyone in the story: it seems to be at some distance both from camp and from town, for it is there that his attendants lay down the wounded Hector after carrying him out of the battle by the ships (14.433), and Achilles turns aside in his pursuit of the fleeing Trojans to kill those who have taken refuge in the river-bed (21.1 ff.), and Hermes leaves Priam to go on without his protection after they have come safely out of the Greek lines (24.692).

There seems to be a slight elevation in the plain, and on this the Trojans array their forces when they prepare for battle after camping on the field (11.56, 20.3). The plain also is furrowed in places by dry stream-beds (16.71). At some distance from both camp and town stands the Tomb of Ilus, a landmark several times mentioned: Agamemnon drives the Trojans in flight past it at the beginning of the third day's battle, and later on the same day, after the Trojans have gained the upper hand, Paris aims his arrow at Diomede from behind its cover (11.166 and 372); at the end of the story Priam and his herald on their way to the Greek camp drive past it before halting to water their beasts in 'the river', presumably Xanthus (24.349).

Also mentioned are two eminences of unspecified location called Callicolōnē and the Fort of Heracles, from which the gods for a time are spectators of the last day's fighting (20.144 ff.). And, also of unspecified location, the Tomb of Aesyētēs, which serves the Trojans as a lookout post (2.793), and a mound on the plain before the town called Batieia or the Tomb of Myrinē, where the Trojans' forces muster before deploying (2.813).

A temporary feature of the scene is a defensive work (wall and ditch with stakes) which the Greeks construct after the first day's fighting (7.436 ff.) for the protection of their camp. We are told rather elaborately (7.443 ff. and 12.4–34) that the gods in displeasure destroyed all trace of it: which implies that local knowledge required an explanation of the absence of ruins in later time. From the manner of its introduction it looks as though the wall was brought into a story which did not at first contain it, in order to make possible the scenes of fighting over it which are subject of Book 12. The Trojans storm it at the end of that book; are driven back over and through it at the beginning of Book 15; and overrun it again later (15.355 ff.), when it is flattened and its ditch filled over a wide stretch by the god Apollo. These events apart it is only occasionally mentioned, though still remembered when Hermes brings Priam and his chariot and waggon into the camp in Book 24 (443 ff.).

In the *Odyssey* the island of Ithaca lies off the NW coast of Peloponnese (4.635, 15.297 etc.). There are other substantial islands in its vicinity (16.247 ff. etc.)—Dulichium, Same (or Samos) and Zacynthus—from which come respectively fifty-two and twenty-four and twenty of Penelope's suitors, twelve more coming from Ithaca itself. The identification of Dulichium and Same is uncertain (? Leucas, now a peninsular, and Cephallenia): Zacynthus and Ithaca are usually and naturally identified with the islands that were so called by the Greeks of the classical period. The description of Ithaca's position in relation to the other islands is confused in the poem: see p. 85 above. But its position in relation to the Greek mainland and Telemachus' journey thither and therefrom corresponds to that of classical Ithaca and is clear enough.

Ithaca is described in the poem as hilly and rocky (4.605 ff., 9.27), without plain-land, but with abundance of springs and timber (13.247), and having as a prominent feature a tree-clad mountain, Mt. Neritos (9.22, 13.351). It is also well provided with harbourage; for in addition to an anchorage near the southern end of the island, where Telemachus lands on his return from Peloponnese (15.36, 495), three harbours are referred to—Rheithron, where Telemachus' visitor at the beginning of the story says he has left his ship 'away from the town' (1.186); the town's harbour, from which Telemachus sets out for Peloponnese (2.382 ff.) and the suitors set out with intent to ambush him on his return (4.669 and 842); and the 'haven of Phorcys' at which Odysseus is landed by his Phaeacian benefactors (13.96 ff.), and which is described as having its entry screened by two crags, steep to seaward and sloping on the landward side.

Near Phorcys' Haven is a cave with two openings and with what seem to have been stalactite formations in its interior, supposed in the story to be household furniture of the nymphs (the fairies, as we might say). Odysseus is instructed by Athena (13.404) to proceed from Phorcys' Haven to the abode of the swineherd Eumaeus, 'near the Raven's Rock and the spring Arethusa'. He makes his way thither over wooded uplands (14.1), and finds the swineherd's hut and fenced farmyard in a clearing with an open view. Thence, as we learn later a difficult track (17.196 and 204) leads to the Ithacan township, nearly half a day's walk away (for it takes Eumaeus a day to carry a message to Penelope and return: 16.2, 130 ff., 452). The way leads over the brow of a hill called Hermes' Hill (16.471), from which there is a view over the town below and its harbour; and it passes a man-made fountain in a grove of trees (17.205 ff.) near to the town, from which the inhabitants are accustomed to fetch their water. In the town itself is Odysseus' own house, with courtyard and double doors and extensive buildings. And outside the town again, in another direction unspecified, is the farmhouse with its verandah and neatly cultivated orchard and vineyard where Laertes in retirement has made his home.

The facts reviewed above invite some observations, namely:

(1) There is a difference between the two poems, *Iliad* and *Odyssey*, in the manner in which locality and landscape are conveyed—a difference due partly, no doubt, to the difference of the subject matter. In the *Iliad* there is hardly any direct description of the physical setting of the story, and the reader only becomes aware of it by the accumulation of casual references to particular features. In the *Odyssey* on

the other hand there is a great deal of quite elaborate description—of Phorcys' Haven, for instance, and the adjoining cave, and the spring in the grove at the approach to the Ithacan town: to create a positive awareness of landscape has been a matter of purpose, conscious or unconscious.

(2) Even in the *Iliad*, where the predominant effect in general is of masses and individuals in combat, and features of the physical *mise en scène* are few and infrequently mentioned, it still appears, from the recurrent though occasional references to certain features, that the poet has a picture of the battlefield and its environment in his own mind's eye. In regard to the *Odyssey*, naturally, this fact is clearer still.

(3) This picture in the poet's mind reflects, in both poems, a correct impression, however derived, of the general geography of the wider area in which the story unfolds, even if here and there the account has been distorted by misinformation or mistransmission. As for detailed features of the scene—the Tomb of Ilus, the Raven's Rock, and so on—these may be real features of a real scene remembered by a poet, or inherited, or imagined, or imported into this story from others in his repertoire: it is impossible now to know, and the explanation may be different in different cases.

But one curious fact deserves to be noted and is provocative of speculation. Archaeologists from the British School at Athens in the 1930s (see F. H. Stubbings in *Companion to Homer*, pp. 418 ff.) discovered on Ithaca in a cave by the sea-shore a number of inscribed sherds showing that the cave in ancient times was sacred to the Nymphs, and also twelve handsome bronze tripods; a thirteenth tripod had been found earlier by the local owner of the land. The tripods appear from their style to have been made in the ninth or eighth century BC. Readers of the *Odyssey* remember that the Phaeacians in the poem give Odysseus thirteen tripods (13.13 ff.: the givers are King Alcinous and twelve lesser princes) and that he stows them away after his arrival in Ithaca in a cave of the Nymphs by the sea-shore (13.217 and 363 ff.).